THE 2012
IRISH
OLYMPIC TEAM
IN LONDON

GO TEAM IRELAND 2012!

OLYMPIC COUNCIL OF IRELAND

Prim-Ed
Publishing
www.prim-ed.com

Official Educational Publisher

2012 Irish Olympic Team in London *Upper (Ages 10+)*

Published by Prim-Ed Publishing® 2011
Copyright© Prim-Ed Publishing® 2011
ISBN 978-1-84654-302-9
PR– 2358

Titles in this series:
2012 Irish Olympic Team in London *Lower (Ages 5–8)*
2012 Irish Olympic Team in London *Middle (Ages 8–10)*
2012 Irish Olympic Team in London *Upper (Ages 10+)*

Internet websites
In some cases, websites or specific URLs may be recommended. While these are checked and rechecked at the time of publication, the publisher has no control over any subsequent changes which may be made to webpages. It is *strongly* recommended that the class teacher checks *all* URLs before allowing pupils to access them.

View all pages online

Website: www.prim-ed.com

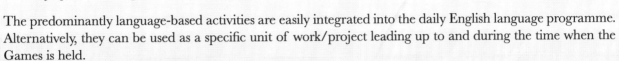

foreword

The London Olympic Games, the Games of the XXX Olympiad or the Summer Olympics, will be held from 27 July to 12 August 2012. This series of books has been written to provide information on:

- *the heritage of the Olympic Games*
- *Ireland's historical and current participation in the Olympic Games*
- *the organisation and sports of the 2012 Olympic Games*
- *the Olympic venues being used throughout London and the UK.*

The predominantly language-based activities are easily integrated into the daily English language programme. Alternatively, they can be used as a specific unit of work/project leading up to and during the time when the Games is held.

Books in this series include:

The 2012 Irish Olympic Team in London (Ages 5–8)
The 2012 Irish Olympic Team in London (Ages 8–10*)*
The 2012 Irish Olympic Team in London (Ages 10+)

Supporting resources include:
- **CD with interactive activities**
- **poster, stickers and door hanger**

contents

teachers notes

The material in this book provides information and activities that will develop a broad understanding of the 2012 Olympic Games. The activities focus on the major learning areas of English but also incorporate other learning areas. The activities have been written to provide fun and enjoyment while learning about the Olympic Games.

The 2012 Irish Olympic Team in London series comprises more than 50 pupil activities and a number of generic activities to complement the theme. The book has been divided into five sections:

- *Olympic Games heritage* – *details of how the Olympic Games began in ancient Greece*
- *Ireland and the Olympic Games* – *includes information about Ireland's past and present participation in the Olympic Games, including important people involved in the Olympic movement; details about the path athletes must take to become Olympians; reference to symbols of Ireland's proud heritage; past and present Irish Olympic sporting legends; and information about the code of ethics of the Irish Sports Council*
- *London Olympic Games* – *covers the organisation and symbols of the Games*
- *Olympic venues* – *information about the facilities and areas being used throughout London and the UK*
- *Sports at the 2012 Olympic Games* – *details of sporting events at the Games*

Each pupil page is supported by a teacher page which provides the following information.

Objective(s) presents the focus of the lesson and the behaviours the pupils should be demonstrating through completion of the activity.

Teacher information provides the teacher with detailed additional information to supplement the pupil page, including information about how to use the worksheet.

Bold words (where included) focus on specific vocabulary in the text. Activities are suggested relating to these and answers are provided if required.

Answers are given where necessary to assist marking.

Additional activities can be used to further develop the focus of the lesson. They provide ideas to consolidate and clarify the concepts and skills taught. The activities cover the same or a different learning area.

Pupil pages are one of three types:

- one page combining both information and pupil activity

OR

- a full page of information about the topic

OR

- a pupil page activity which is used in conjunction with the full page of pupil information. These pages may include comprehension questions, retrieval or research activities or another fun activity.

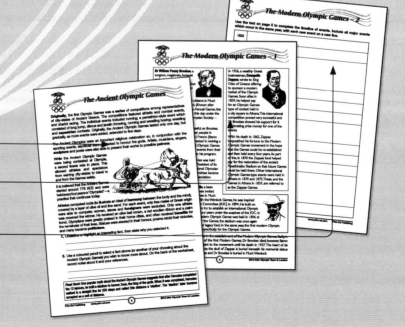

teachers notes

The generic pupil pages at the front of the book can be used at the teacher's discretion, either several times throughout the Games or once as required. Activities can be modified to suit pupil ability levels. Explanations of the pages are given below.

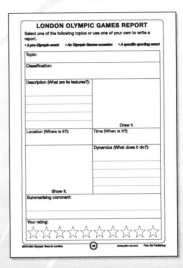

Athlete profile and performance

(page vi)

Allows pupils the opportunity to consider which athlete they admire, to research his or her life and to follow his or her progress at the Games.

Record of results

(page vii)

Provides pupils with a spreadsheet to track the progress of their 15 favourite countries at the Games.

London Games report

(page viii)

Specifically designed to be used for anything related to the London Games, whether it be a venue, event, presentation, ceremony, equipment or occasion.

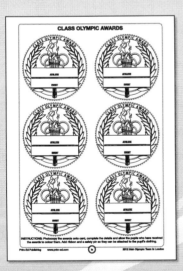

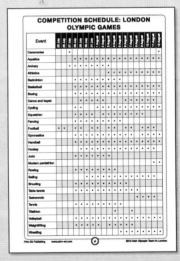

Class Olympic awards

(page ix)

Specifically designed to be used for any activities completed during the time the London Games are held. This could be a sporting or an academic activity.

Modern Olympic Games information

(page x)

Useful teacher background information which can be used to inform pupils or generate ideas and activities for the class or pupils. Useful website references are also included.

Competition schedule

(page xi)

Included to provide an easy reference of the timetable for the Games. Teachers or pupils could devise questions to answer when reading the schedule.

ATHLETE PROFILE AND PERFORMANCE

Complete this chart about an athlete of your choice.

Name:	
Date of birth:	
Birthplace:	
Sport:	
Occupation:	Picture of athlete
Sporting achievements:	

London Olympic Games Performance

Event	Result	Comment

Summary of performance:

RECORD OF RESULTS

Select 15 countries and keep a tally of their results during the *London Olympic Games*.

Country	Medals			Total
	Gold	Silver	Bronze	

LONDON OLYMPIC GAMES REPORT

Select one of the following topics or use one of your own to write a report.

• *A pre-Olympic event*   • *An Olympic Games occasion*   • *A specific sporting event*

Topic:

Classification:

Description (What are its features?):

Draw it

Location (Where is it?):

Time (When is it?):

Dynamics (What does it do?):

Show it.

Summarising comment:

Your rating:

CLASS OLYMPIC AWARDS

INSTRUCTIONS: Photocopy the awards onto card, complete the details and allow the pupils who have received the awards to colour them. Add ribbon and a safety pin so they can be attached to the pupil's clothing.

MODERN OLYMPIC GAMES INFORMATION

YEAR	HOST CITY	COUNTRY	MASCOT(S)
1896	Athens	Greece	—
1900	Paris	France	—
1904	St. Louis	USA	—
1908	London	United Kingdom	—
1912	Stockholm	Sweden	—
1916	Cancelled due to World War I		—
1920	Antwerp	Belgium	—
1924	Paris	France	—
1928	Amsterdam	Netherlands	—
1932	Los Angeles	USA	—
1936	Berlin	Germany	—
1940	Cancelled due to World War II		—
1944	Cancelled due to World War II		—
1948	London	United Kingdom	—
1952	Helsinki	Finland	—
1956	Melbourne	Australia	—
1960	Rome	Italy	—
1964	Tokyo	Japan	—
1968	Mexico City	Mexico	Red jaguar and a dove
1972	Munich	Germany	Waldi, a dachshund
1976	Montreal	Canada	Amik, the beaver
1980	Moscow	USSR	Misha, the bear cub
1984	Los Angeles	USA	Sam, the bald eagle
1988	Seoul	South Korea	Hodori and Hosuni, two tiger cubs
1992	Barcelona	Spain	Cobi, a Catalan sheepdog
1996	Atlanta	USA	Izzy, an abstract figure
2000	Sydney	Australia	Olly, the kookaburra; Syd, the platypus; Millie, the echidna
2004	Athens	Greece	Athena and Phevos, two ancient Greek dolls—a brother and sister
2008	Beijing	China	The five Friendlies—Beibei, the fish; Jingjing, the panda; Huanhuan, the Olympic flame; Yingying, the Tibetan antelope; and Nini, the swallow
2012	London	United Kingdom	Wenlock (Mandeville is the Paralympic Mascot)—drops of steel
(Scheduled) 2016	Rio de Janeiro	Brazil	unknown

- For a list, explanation and images of all emblems for Summer Olympic Games from 1932 onwards, go to <http://www.athensinfoguide.com/olympicemblemssummer.htm>.

- For images and explanations of Olympic torches for each Olympic Games since 1936, go to <http://www.athensinfoguide.com/olympictorchessummer.htm>.

NOTE: The 1906 Summer Olympics held in Athens (also called the 1906 Intercalated Games) has not been included in this list as it is not officially recognised by the International Olympic Committee.

COMPETITION SCHEDULE: LONDON OLYMPIC GAMES

Event	25 July	26 July	27 July	28 July	29 July	30 July	31 July	1 August	2 August	3 August	4 August	5 August	6 August	7 August	8 August	9 August	10 August	11 August	12 August
Ceremonies			•																•
Aquatics				•	•	•	•	•	•	•	•	•	•	•	•	•	•	•	•
Archery			•	•	•	•	•	•	•	•									
Athletics										•	•	•	•	•	•	•	•	•	•
Badminton				•	•	•	•	•	•	•	•	•							
Basketball				•	•	•	•	•	•	•		•	•	•	•	•	•	•	•
Boxing				•	•	•	•	•	•	•	•		•	•	•	•	•	•	•
Canoe and kayak					•	•	•	•	•			•	•	•	•	•	•	•	
Cycling					•	•			•	•	•	•	•	•	•	•			
Equestrian				•	•	•	•		•	•	•	•	•	•	•	•			
Fencing				•	•	•		•	•	•	•	•							
Football	•	•		•	•		•	•		•	•		•	•		•	•	•	
Gymnastics				•	•	•	•	•	•	•	•	•	•	•		•	•	•	•
Handball				•	•	•	•	•	•	•	•	•	•	•	•	•	•	•	•
Hockey					•	•	•	•	•	•	•	•	•	•	•	•	•	•	
Judo				•	•	•	•	•	•	•									
Modern pentathlon																		•	•
Rowing				•	•	•	•	•	•	•	•								
Sailing						•	•	•	•	•	•	•	•	•	•	•	•	•	
Shooting				•	•	•	•	•	•	•	•	•							
Table tennis				•	•	•	•	•	•	•	•	•	•	•	•				
Taekwondo															•	•	•	•	
Tennis				•	•	•	•	•	•	•	•	•							
Triathlon											•			•					
Volleyball				•	•	•	•	•	•	•	•	•	•	•	•	•	•	•	•
Weightlifting				•	•	•		•		•	•	•	•	•					
Wrestling												•	•	•	•	•	•	•	•

the ancient olympic games

objective

- Reads information and completes activities about the Ancient Olympic Games.

teacher information

- The Ancient Olympic games were only one of four Panhellenic Games held in honour of the gods. The others were the Pythian Games at Delphi, the Isthmian Games at Corinth and the Nemean Games at Nemea. Zeus was honoured at both the Olympian and Nemean Games, Apollo at Delphi, and Poseidon at Isthmia.

- The Ancient Olympic Games came to a halt in 393 CE, when the Roman emperor Theodosius II, who ruled Greece at the time, wanted to spread the Christian religion.

- The first olive wreath crown is believed to have been made from leaves taken from a sacred tree growing near the temple of Zeus at Olympia.

- In his home city, a victorious Olympian may have received free housing and meals, and coins with the athlete's image on them were often made. This meant he became known throughout the ancient Greek empire. It was believed that a victory brought glory to an athlete's city, much as it does today.

bold words

- Use a dictionary to find the meaning of the bold words:

  originally – *at first, to start with*

  series – *a number of events or things in a sequence*

  equestrian – *relating to horse riding or riders*

  sculptors – *people who practise the art of sculpting (the art of creating figures or designs in relief, or by cutting marble, wood, granite; by modelling in clay, or by making moulds for casting in bronze or other metal)*

  patrons – *people who support or protect an artist, person, institution or enterprise*

  truce – *a suspension of hostilities, as between armies, by agreement, for a specified period; an armistice*

  harmony – *agreement, accord*

  foreigners – *people not native to the country*

  benefits – *advantages, acts of kindness*

  politicians – *people involved in political government or administration, or public office*

answers

Teacher check

additional activities

- Read other myths and legends from Ancient Greece, then sketch a scene or character from one.

- Visit <*http://www.olympic.org/results?q=ancient%20 olympic%20games*> to download a PDF of interesting information about *The Olympic Games in Antiquity*. This booklet gives background information about the training and preparation of Ancient Olympians for the Games.

- Research Richard Chandler, an English traveller who discovered the site of ancient Olympia. Find out what details about the Ancient Olympic Games were unearthed.

The Ancient Olympic Games

Originally, the first Olympic Games was a **series** of competitions among representatives of city-states of Ancient Greece. The competitions featured athletic and combat events, and chariot racing. The individual events included running; a pentathlon-style event which consisted of long jump, discus and javelin throwing, running and wrestling; boxing; wrestling; and **equestrian** contests. Originally, the Ancient Olympic Games lasted only one day, but gradually, as more events were added, extended to five days.

The Ancient Olympics were an important religious celebration so, in conjunction with the sporting events, sacrifices were presented to honour the gods. Artists, musicians, singers, **sculptors** and poets were also able to present their works to possible **patrons**.

While the Ancient Olympic Games were being contested at Olympia, a sacred **truce** was in place. This allowed athletes and spectators from warring city-states to travel to and from the Games safely.

It is believed that the Ancient Games started around 776 BCE and were held every four years or 'Olympiad' — a practice that continues today.

Athletes competed nude (to illustrate an ideal of **harmony** between the body and the mind), covered by a layer of olive oil and fine sand. Only free males of Greek origin were able to compete; women, slaves and **foreigners** were excluded. For each event, only one athlete was crowned the winner. He received an olive leaf crown, a red woollen ribbon and a palm frond. Olympians were greatly praised in their home cities, and often received **benefits** for the remainder of their lives. Statues were erected in their honour, poems retold their victories, and many became **politicians**.

1. Underline or highlight an interesting fact, then state why you selected it.

_____

_____

2. Use a coloured pencil to select a fact above (or another of your choosing about the Ancient Olympic Games) you wish to know more about. On the back of the worksheet, record notes about it and your references.

_____

_____

> **_Fast fact:_** One popular myth about the Ancient Olympic Games suggests that after Hercules completed the 12 labours, he built a stadium to honour Zeus, the king of the gods. When it was completed, Hercules walked in a straight line for 200 steps and called this distance a 'stadion'. The 'stadion' later became accepted as a unit of distance.

OLYMPIC COUNCIL OF IRELAND

the modern olympic games

objective

- Reads information and completes activities about the development of the Modern Olympic Games.

teacher information

- Some earlier versions of the Modern Olympic Games were held in 1612 in the Cotswolds, England, and annually in France from 1796 to 1798. Interesting facts about the Cotswold Olimpick Games can be found at <http://www.chippingcampdenonline.org/ Chipping-Campden/robert-dovers-cotswold-olimpick-games.html> and at <http://www.olimpickgames.co.uk/>.

- After visiting England and seeing organised sport Baron Pierre de Coubertin believed that exercise was an important part of developing well-educated, well-rounded individuals. At first his desire to encourage more sport in France was not met with enthusiasm, but he persisted and, because he had influence, his opinions began to take root. He organised the International Olympic Games Committee and at its first meeting, with seven delegates from nine countries, members voted unanimously to resurrect the Olympic Games.

- The connection to Much Wenlock was the reason the mascot for the London Games was named Wenlock. Visit the Wenlock Games website at <http://www.wenlock-olympian-society.org.uk/> to research how the Games are still held.

bold words

The words in bold print are the names of three prominent people in the establishment of the Modern Olympic Games. For each person, write bullet point notes about their major contributions and research other interesting facts about them. Both could be given as an oral presentation.

answers

Page 6

	Answers for page 6
1850	• In 1850, Dr William Penny Brookes starts an annual games of 'an Olympian class' for local citizens in Much Wenlock, Shropshire, England.
1856	• A wealthy Greek businessman, Evangelis Zappas, writes to King Otto of Greece offering to sponsor a modern revival of the Ancient Olympic Games.
1859	• An Olympic Games-type contest, sponsored by Zappas, is held in a city square in Athens. • Dr Brookes donates prize money to the Games. • The games in Much Wenlock are renamed the Wenlock Society Annual Games.
1860	• Dr William Penny Brookes founds the Wenlock Olympian Society.
1865	• Evangelis Zappas dies and leaves his fortune to help fund the Modern Olympic Games in the hope they will occur every four years.
1866	• A national Olympic Games is held in London with Dr Brookes as the president of its organising committee: the National Olympian Association.
1870	• The Zappas fund helps pay for restoration of the Panathinaiko Stadium. • Second Zappas games are held in Athens, Greece.
1875	• Third Zappas Games are held in Athens, Greece.
1890	• Baron Pierre de Coubertin visits Dr William Penny Brookes at Much Wenlock.
1894	• Baron Pierre de Coubertin founds the International Olympic Committee (IOC).
1895	• Dr William Penny Brookes dies.
1896	• The First Modern Olympic Games is held in Athens, Greece. • The Panathinaiko Stadium is again refurbished using Zappas' legacy fund. • The first modern Olympic building, the Zappeion, is built.
1937	• Baron Pierre de Coubertin dies.

Page 7

Refer to page x in the front pages for information. Note: 1916, 1940 and 1944 have been included so that the pupils can discover that Games were not held in these years due to World Wars I and II.

additional activities

- Research to find out how new sports are added to the Modern Olympic Games programme.

- Use a table and the information on pages 2 and 3 to compare the Ancient and Modern Olympic Games.

- On a large sheet of art paper, write the decorative heading 'The Modern Olympic Games', then use sketches and internet-sourced images to display information in illustration form about the Modern Olympic Games.

Dr William Penny Brookes, a surgeon, magistrate, botanist and educator, campaigned strongly for physical education to be included in the school curriculum. In 1850, he staged an annual games of

'an Olympian Class' for local citizens in Much Wenlock, Shropshire, England. (Known after 1859 as the Wenlock Society Annual Games, this sporting festival continues to this day under the direction of the Wenlock Olympian Society—founded in 1860.)

The games proved very successful, so Brookes, over a length of time, contacted people in Greece (Evangelis Zappas) and France (Baron de Coubertin) who were interested in reviving a modern version of the Ancient Olympic Games. He also included some athletic events from their Olympic-type sports contests to his programme.

In 1866, a national Olympic Games was held in London with Dr Brookes as President of its organising committee—the National Olympian Association. Much later, this committee became known as the British Olympic Association.

In 1956, a wealthy Greek businessman, **Evangelis Zappas**, wrote to King Otto of Greece offering to sponsor a modern revival of the Olympic Games. Soon after, in 1859, he helped pay for an Olympic Games-type of contest held in

a city square in Athens. This international competition proved very successful and Dr Brookes showed his support for it by donating prize money for one of the events.

With his death in 1865, Zappas bequeathed his fortune to the Modern Olympic Games movement in the hope that the Games could be re-established and then held every four years. As part of this, in 1870, the Zappas fund helped pay for the restoration of the ancient Panathinaiko Stadium so that future Games could be held there. Other international Olympic Games-type events were held in Athens in 1870 and 1875. These, and the Games in Athens in 1859, are referred to as the Zappas Games.

In 1890, **Baron Pierre de Coubertin**, a keen supporter of sport in education, was invited by Dr Brookes to attend the Games in Much Wenlock. Being very impressed with the Wenlock Games, he was inspired to found the International Olympic Committee (IOC) in 1894. He built on the ideas of Brookes and Zappas to try to establish an international Olympic Games which would occur every four years under the auspices of the IOC. In keeping with its origins, the first Modern Olympic Games was held in 1896 at Panathinaiko Stadium in Athens. For the Games, the stadium was once again refurbished using funds from Zappas' legacy fund. In the same year, the first modern Olympic building—the Zappeion—was built specifically for the Olympic Games.

All three men played an important role in the establishment of the Modern Olympic Games. Sadly, in 1895, four months before the staging of the first Modern Games, Dr Brookes died; however, Baron de Coubertin continued to be important to the movement until his death in 1937. The heart of de Coubertin is buried at Olympia, Greece; the skull of Zappas is buried beneath his memorial statue outside the Zappeion in Athens, Greece; and Dr Brookes is buried in Much Wenlock.

The Modern Olympic Games – 2

Use the text on page 5 to complete the timeline of events. Include all major events which occur in the same year, with each new event on a new line.

1850	
1856	
1859	
1860	
1865	
1866	
1870	
1875	
1890	
1894	
1895	
1896	
1937	

The Modern Olympic Games – 3

Use the following websites to help complete the table about the Summer Olympic Games.

- *<http://www.topendsports.com/events/summer/hosts/list.htm>*
- *<http://www.the-sports.org/olympics-s16-c0-b0.html>*

Year	Host City	Country	Year	Host City	Country
1896			1956		
1900			1960		
1904			1964		
1908			1968		
1912			1972		
1916			1976		
1920			1980		
1924			1984		
1928			1988		
1932			1992		
1936			1996		
1940			2000		
1944			2004		
1948			2008		
1952			2012		

the olympic Rings

objective

- Reads and demonstrates understanding of text by selecting and summarising information to write sentences.

teacher information

- One of most recognisable symbols in the world is the Olympic Flag with its five interlocking rings of blue, black, red, yellow and green on a white background. It was adopted by the International Olympic Committee in 1914.

- The 1916 Games were cancelled because of the First World War, so the flag was not used until the 1920 Games in Antwerp, Belgium. The Rings first appeared with regularity on posters for the Winter Olympics in 1928. The symbol was especially popular during the Games in Berlin in 1936 and it is now synonymous with the Summer and Winter Olympics and is found on promotional materials and publications.

- It was stated in the official Olympic handbook that each continent was represented by a particular colour of a ring, but as there was no evidence that this was what de Corbertin had intended, it was removed in 1951.

- The Olympic Rings reinforce the idea that the Olympic movement is international and welcomes all countries. Baron de Coubertin is quoted as saying, 'These five rings represent the five parts of the world which now are won over to Olympism and willing to accept healthy competition'.

- Replicas of the Olympic Rings were put on display at St Pancras Station in London, 17 months before the 2012 Games. Visitors arriving in London via the Channel Tunnel train are greeted by the huge, 20 m-by-9 m aluminium rings suspended from the roof. There are also plans for them to feature on the London Eye and as an LED light display on Tower Bridge. (LED uses less energy, so is consistent with the 'Sustainable Games' concept.)

- Visit <http://news.bbc.co.uk/sport2/hi/olympics/london_2012/7577999.stm> for information about the handover of the Olympic Flag to London at the Beijing Olympic Closing Ceremony.

answers

1. The five interlocking rings should be coloured blue, black, red from the top left, then yellow and green underneath.
2. Teacher check

additional activities

- Compile a list of different places where the Olympic Rings are displayed and the objects which have this symbol on them.

- Research Baron de Coubertin and write 10 interesting facts about him and his life. Share the information with the class.

- Study the way the five Olympic Rings are linked. Write a detailed description and explain what this symbolises.

- Design your own Olympic Flag and write an explanation of what it represents.

The Olympic Rings

The Olympic Flag, with its five rings of blue, black, red, yellow and green on a white background, was designed after the 1912 Games by the founder of the modern Olympics, a Frenchman named Baron Pierre de Coubertin.

The five Olympic Rings represent the five inhabited continents of Europe, Asia, Australia, Africa and the Americas. Baron de Coubertin designed the rings to reflect the international nature of the Games. He believed it was very important that every country accepted friendly competition and that they all felt welcome to become part of the Olympics. At least one of the Olympic Rings' five colours appears on every national flag.

Throughout the world today, the Olympic Rings are the symbol of Olympic competition. They can be seen everywhere before and during the Games: on posters, publications, signs, tickets, websites and advertising materials. However, it wasn't until the Berlin Games in 1936 that these five linked rings became such a recognisable and important part of both the Summer and Winter Olympics.

The Olympic Flag, with its white background and simple but effective symbol of the five rings linking the continents of the world, is raised at the Opening Ceremony and flown at the Olympic Stadium throughout the Games. At the Closing Ceremony, the mayor of the current host city hands the flag to the president of the International Olympic Committee who then presents it to the mayor of the next Olympic host city.

1. Trace the first ring and use it as a template to complete the drawing of the Olympic flag, then colour it appropriately.

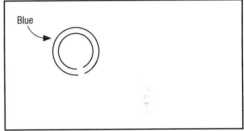

2. Complete an interesting sentence for each aspect of the Olympic Rings.

(a) *History* • Baron Pierre de Coubertin _____

_____

_____

(b) *Description* • The Olympic Flag _____

_____

_____

(c) *Symbolism* • The Olympic Rings symbolise _____

_____

_____

(d) *London* • In London, the Olympic Rings _____

_____

_____

the olympic torch

objective

- Reads and researches information about the Olympic torch to complete an information chart.

teacher information

- In ancient Greece, perpetual fires were burnt in front of important temples. Such a fire was created by a circular mirror (called a skaphia) focussing the sun's rays to produce a point of intense heat which set fire to wood or dry grass. This was done to ensure the purity of the fire. There was no torch relay at the Ancient Olympics but a race (called the *lampadedromia*) determined who had the honour of renewing the fire in the cauldron at ceremonies to honour certain gods in Athens.

- At modern-day Olympic flame lighting ceremonies, a skaphia is again used to ignite the flame. This flame is used by the high priestess to light the first runner's torch from an urn. Some 'backup' flames are also created.

- Although an Olympic Cauldron has been used since 1928, it was the Secretary General of the 1936 Olympic Organising Committee, a German historian called Carl Diem, who introduced the Olympic Torch Relay. This torch was carried by elite German athletes from Greece through most of the countries of Europe to Berlin. There are suggestions that the motives behind this first Torch Relay may have been political.

- The Olympic Torch Relay has become an integral part of the Olympics and is a message of peace and friendship. A host country uses the Relay to showcase landmarks and places of interest to the world. The event is supported by sponsors who organise it and cover the costs. In the past, it has also been a focus for protest with previous examples including those protesting China's human rights policy in the lead-up to the Beijing Games, and those concerned about indigenous land rights in Canada.

- The Olympic Torch for the 2012 Games arrives in the United Kingdom on 19 May 2012. It has 8000 holes to represent the number of torchbearers who will carry it. For this reason it has been referred to by some Britons as the 'Cheese Grater'.

- Visit <*http://www.youtube.com/watch?v=OrV1R7iAzXI*> to view the 2008 reenactment of the lighting of the Olympic torch ceremony at Olympia.

- Visit <*http://www.nytimes.com/interactive/2008/08/01/sports/20080802_TORCH_GRAPHIC.html*> to view images and information about all the Olympic torches from 1936 to 2008.

- Visit <*http://www.olympic.org/Documents/Reports/EN/len_report_655.pdf*> to read about the Olympic Flame and Torch Relay.

answers

Teacher check

additional activities

- Discuss and make a list of the many different ways fire is used and how important it is to human life. Decide if the ancient Greeks were justified in valuing it as they did and believing it had sacred qualities.

- Research and write a report about an athlete who was given the honour of lighting the Olympic Cauldron when his or her country hosted an Olympic Games.

- Find an illustration of an Olympic Torch, research what its design represents and make a careful copy of it. Label and briefly explain its relevant features.

The Olympic Torch

The Olympic Torch provides a link between the Ancient and Modern Games. Ancient Greeks believed fire had sacred qualities and that it was given to humans by the god Prometheus, who stole it from Zeus. So during Ancient Olympic Games (starting in 776 BCE), a sacred flame was burnt on the altar of Hestia as a sign of purity, peace and reason. Heralds of Peace were sent out in relays to let everyone know there was a sacred truce and that they could travel to the Olympics in safety.

However, when the Modern Olympic Games started in 1896 there was no Torch or Cauldron; they had been forgotten. The Cauldron was reintroduced in Amsterdam in 1928 and the Torch Relay in 1936, when it was taken through Europe from Greece to Berlin. The Torch is lit by a flame produced by the sun's rays in a curved mirror, in front of Hera's temple at Mount Olympia. The Flame is then placed in an urn, taken to an ancient stadium and used to light the first Torch.

The Torch is different for every games and has to be designed by the host nation. It often reflects that Games' theme and some aspect of the host nation. It must also be carefully tested to meet strict requirements. It must be very light, have a flame at the top which lasts and burns brightly, be able to withstand all types of weather and it must be safe. Some early torches used olive oil, resin or gunpowder, but modern torches use gas. However, there have been some disasters along the way. The magnesium and aluminum used in the 1956 torches fell out and burnt the arms of torchbearers. There are many thousands of torches needed for the relay. Torchbearers are permitted to purchase their Torch after finishing their part of the relay.

Olympic Torches have been carried by runners and people in wheelchairs; they have been transported by horse, camel, snowmobile, dogsled, parachute, boat, plane and even been taken underwater at Australia's Great Barrier Reef. Many torchbearers are athletes, but others who have served their community well are also often chosen for this honour. The greatest honour is given to the host nation's athlete(s) who enter the Olympic Stadium, do a lap of honour and light the Cauldron at the Opening Ceremony.

Use the information given to compare ancient and modern Olympic Torch Relays.

Ancient Olympics	Modern Olympics

the olympic medals

objectives

- Reads and comprehends information about the history of Summer Olympic Games medals.
- Researches to summarise past and present designs of Summer Olympic Games medals.

teacher information

- The first ever medals were based on ancient Roman coins that the scholarly and wealthy collected. The front of the coin (obverse) usually showed a portrait and the back showed a virtue or quality of that person.

- Olympic medals are awarded during a medal presentation following the final of each event. The gold, silver and bronze medal winners stand on a three-tiered podium, with the gold medal winner(s) standing on the highest of the three tiers. The bronze medal(s) is/are awarded first, followed by the silver medal(s) and finally the gold medal(s). A medal attached to a ribbon is placed around each athlete's neck by an IOC (International Olympic Committee) official. The national flags of the three medallists are raised (gold medal winner in the highest position) and the national anthem of the gold medallist is played.

bold words

- Sort the bold words into parts of speech; e.g. proper nouns, common nouns, verbs.

  proper nouns – *Athens, Paris, Greek, Panathinaikon Stadium, St Louis, Amsterdam, Munich, London*

  common nouns – *medals, diameter, image*

  conjunction – *until*

  verbs – *participated, minting*

  adverb – *currently*

  adjectives – *ancient, specific, next, commemorative*

- Locate all the bold words that are cities on a map of the world.

answers

St. Louis 1904: Nike (Greek goddess personifying victory) on one side, athlete holding laurel crown and relief of ancient sports on the other; 3.5 mm thick and 37.8 mm diam.

Amsterdam 1928: Giuseppe Cassioli wins IOC competition to design medals. Basic design remains same from 1928 to 1968. Nike on one side, seated with winner carried by crowd on other; 3 mm thick and 55 mm diam.

Munich 1972: Nike design same as before, mythical Greek twin sons Pollux and Castor on back; 6.5 mm thick and 66 mm diam.

London 2012: Largest medal to date; Nike is in standing position, and modern symbolic imagery on other side with a 'grid' and River Thames theme as a ribbon; 7 mm thick, 85 mm diam.

additional activities

- Pupils can use the websites listed on the worksheet to view the Olympic medals of the modern era. They can then complete the following activities:

  – The medals had the same design from the 1928 Games to the 1968 Games. Compare the differences in colour and size during this period.

  – Each pupil decides on his or her favourite medal. Pupil then describes the design in detail and why he or she liked that medal the best.

  – Find out about the ancient Greek gods, goddesses or buildings depicted on the medals; e.g. Nike, twins Pollux and Castor, Panathinaikon Stadium.

The Olympic medals

Olympic medals were not awarded at the **ancient** Olympic Games. Winners were presented with an olive wreath, which was worn on the head. At the first Modern Olympic Games in **Athens** in 1896, and the **next** Olympic Games in **Paris** in 1900, winners received a silver medal, an olive branch and a certificate. Second placegetters were presented with a bronze medal, a laurel branch and a certificate. Third placegetters did not receive an award. All athletes who **participated** in the Games received a **commemorative** medal.

Gold, silver and bronze **medals** for first, second and third place were not awarded **until** the 1904 Olympic Games in St. Louis, USA. Since those Games, the designs and sizes have changed over time. The International Olympic Committee (IOC) has **specific** guidelines for the design of the medals, of which it is the host city's responsibility for gaining approval by the IOC and for **minting** the medals. **Currently**, gold and silver medals must be 97.5 per cent silver (plated with 6 g of gold for the gold medal) and the bronze medal composed of 97 per cent copper. All medals must be at least 60 mm in **diameter** and 3 mm thick. The obverse (front) of the medal has Nike, the Greek goddess of victory, standing holding a wreath in one hand and a palm leaf in the other. An **image** of the **Greek Panathinaikon Stadium** is included. The host city designs the reverse side.

1896 Olympic Games medal

Front   Back

Research to find out about the design and other facts of some of the past and present Olympic medals. Use bullet points, keywords and phrases to summarise the information. (One box has been left blank for you to choose an Olympic Games of your own.) The following websites will help you:

- *<http://www.athensinfoguide.com/ olympicmedalssummer.htm>*

- *<http://www.bbc.co.uk/news/uk- 14291544>*

- *<http://www.london2012.com/ news/2011/07/olympic-medals-unveiled- to-the-world.php>.*

St. Louis 1904	
Amsterdam 1928	
Munich 1972	
London 2012	

OLYMPIC COUNCIL OF IRELAND

irish olympic history

objective
- Reads information and completes activities about the history of Irish involvement in the Olympic Games.

teacher information
- In 1952, the Irish Olympic Council became the Olympic Council of Ireland to reinforce the fact that it represented the whole island rather than just the Republic of Ireland.

- At the Winter Olympic Games, Ireland has competed in bobsleigh, alpine and cross-country skiing, and skeleton. The best result was obtained by Clifton Wrottesley, who came fourth in skeleton in 2002.

- The official website of the Olympic Council of Ireland is <http://www.olympicsport.ie/>.

- The total number of medals Ireland has won at Olympic Games between 1924 and 2008 are: 8 gold, 7 silver and 8 bronze. Before that time, any medals won by Irish athletes were added to the United Kingdom's total.

bold words
Page 15
Research to find out the official name of Great Britain, what the hammer throw event entails, what the role of the OCI is, and when Winter Olympic Games are held. Refer to <https://www.cia.gov/library/publications/the-world-factbook/geos/uk.html>, <http://hammerthrow.org/what-is-the-hammer/>, <http://www.olympicsport.ie/about/3019-presidents-welcome.html> and <http://teacher.scholastic.com/researchtools/researchstarters/olympics/> for assistance.

Page 16
Use a dictionary to find out the meaning of the words, then explain the difference to a classmate. Answers may be similar to: expulsion—the act of driving out or away; boycotts—actions of groups or individuals who combine to abstain from something in order to intimidate or coerce someone else to do something; opposition—the action of opposing, resisting or combating.

Page 17
Place the bold words into alphabetical order. The order is: Association, became, career, committee, competitors, Council, duties, elected, excelled, executive, federations, four.

answers
Page 15
1. Great Britain and Ireland, 1920
2. The Olympic Council of Ireland was established.
3. Ireland attended the Games under its own name.
4. 1928
5. 1992
6. Ireland has attended every Summer Olympic Games since 1924.
7. The OCI decided to allow athletes both in Northern Ireland to compete for either the United Kingdom or Ireland.

Page 16
(a) son	(b) title
(c) educated	(d) enjoyed
(e) rugby	(f) service
(g) British	(h) author
(i) rural	(j) administration
(k) Ireland	(l) Vice-President
(m) retired	(n) movement
(o) Life	(p) issues
(q) political	(r) drugs

Page 17
1. Four: the OCI, the IOC, the ANOC and the EOC. (He only dealt with SLOOC and was not a member of it.)
2.–3. Teacher check

additional activities
- Research to find which Irish athletes won Olympic medals while a part of the United Kingdom team before 1924. Try OCI history at <http://www.olympicsport.ie/about/3022-oci-history.html>.

Irish Olympic history – 1

Use the time line of information about Ireland's involvement in the Olympic Games to complete the answers.

YEAR(S)	EVENT
1896–1920	Ireland attended Olympic Games as part of the **Great Britain** and Ireland team.
1922	Olympic Council of Ireland established.
1924	Ireland attends Paris Olympic Games under its own name for the first time.
1928	Pat O'Callaghan wins gold medal in the **hammer throw** athletics event.
1924–2008	Ireland attends every Summer Olympic Games.
1952	**Olympic Council of Ireland (OCI)** allows athletes born in Northern Ireland to compete for Ireland or for the United Kingdom.
1992–2010	Ireland attends **Winter Olympic Games**.

1. Ireland competed as part of the _____ team from

during the years of 1896 to _____.

2. What important event in Irish Olympic history happened in 1922?

_____

_____

3. What happened at the Paris 1924 Olympic Games?

_____

4. In what year did Ireland win its first Olympic medal?

_____

5. In which year did Ireland first enter the Winter

Olympic Games?_____

6. What is Ireland's record of attendance at Summer Olympic Games?

_____

_____

7. What decision was made by the OCI in 1952?_____

Fast fact: Irish athletes have won Olympic medals in the sports of athletics, boxing, sailing and swimming at the Summer Olympics.

Irish Olympic history – 2

1. Complete the information about Lord Killanin, an important person in Irish Olympic history. Use the words provided in the box.

Vice-President	**retired**	**Ireland**	**author**	**rugby**	**rural**
administration	**political**	**British**	**service**	**Life**	**son**
educated	**movement**	**enjoyed**	**issues**	**title**	**drugs**

Michael Morris was born in London on 30 July 1914, the ______________[a] of an officer in the Irish Guards and an Australian mother. In 1927, he inherited the ______________[b] of Lord Killanin from an uncle. He was ______________[c] at Eton College, the Sorbonne and Cambridge University. He ______________[d] playing sports—in particular, boxing, rowing, ______________[e] and, later, horse racing.

Lord Killanin volunteered for British military ______________[f] in 1938 and was later awarded an MBE (Member of the Order of the ______________[g] Empire). His extensive career included being a reporter and political correspondent, ______________[h] and film producer. One film he collaborated on, *The Quiet Man*, created a very favourable image of Irish ______________[i] life and helped boost tourism in Ireland. In 1950, he took up his first sports ______________[j] role as President of the Olympic Council of ______________[k].He became a member of the International Olympic Committee (IOC) in 1952 and, in 1967, was elected to its board. He became first ______________[l] in 1968. In 1972 he became President of the IOC, a position he held until he ______________[m] in 1980. For his service to the Olympic ______________[n], he was awarded the Olympic Order in Gold, and was elected Honorary President for ______________[o] of the Olympic Council of Ireland. During his time as President of the OCI of Ireland, he had to deal with many difficult ______________[p], including the **expulsion** of athletes and teams, and **boycotts** of and **opposition** to the Games by nations for ______________[q] reasons. At the time of his retirement, he held grave concerns for athletes as the use of performance-enhancing ______________[r] became more common. He died in Dublin on 25 April 1999.

2. Re-read the completed cloze information text.

Read the text then answer the questions.

Patrick Joseph Hickey was born in Dublin in 1945. When he was younger, he **excelled** in the sport of judo and was chosen to represent Ireland internationally.

His **career** in sports administration is quite extensive. For many years, he was an executive of the European Judo Union. Because of his links with the sport, he has received the title of honorary Life President of the Irish Judo **Association**. In 1984, he was the manager of the Irish Olympic Team that attended the Los Angeles Olympic Games.

In 1988, he was elected Chef de Mission of the Irish team for the Seoul Olympic Games. This means he was elected by his national Olympic **committee**, the Olympic Council of Ireland (OCI), to represent Ireland when dealing with the International Olympic Committee (IOC), the international **federations** of various Olympic sports and the Seoul Olympic Organising Committee (SLOOC). He also had to perform any other **duties** assigned to him by the OCI, such as looking after the welfare of all Irish **competitors** and officials. He held the same role for Ireland at the 1992 Barcelona Olympic Games.

Since 1989, he has continued to be re-elected every **four** years to be President of the Olympic **Council** of Ireland.

In 1994, he **became** a member of the **executive** board of the Association of National Olympic Committees (ANOC) and became its Vice-President in 2006.

In 1995, he became a member of the International Olympic Committee and has held various roles within the organisation since.

From 1997 to 2001, he was Vice-President of the European Olympic Committee (EOC). He was **elected** Secretary General of the EOC in 2001 and, in 2006, he was elected President of the EOC. This is a role he continues to perform to this day.

In the years leading up to the 2016 Rio de Janeiro Olympic Games, he will take on a prominent role in their organisation.

1. How many different Olympic committees has Pat Hickey been in, or is still, a part of?

_____

2. How important is the role of a sports administrator to the organisation and smooth running of an Olympic Games? Explain your opinion.

_____

_____

3. List some skills needed by a person to fulfil the jobs Pat Hickey has; for example good communication skills.

```



```

what does it take to Be an olympian?

OBJECTIVE

• Reads information and answers questions about the requirements and training to become an Olympic athlete.

teacher information

• Pages 19 and 20 should be used together.

• Each country and national sporting association has its own method of selecting athletes for an Olympics team. Generally, athletes must be a member of the national governing body of their chosen sport, and attend national championships. Athletes in team sports are usually chosen by the national coaching squad, having gained a reputation through national competitions or previous competitions. Athletes in individual sports must compete for a position in an Olympic team through qualifying tournaments, trials or national rankings.

• Although the International Olympic Committee (IOC) does not recognise or endorse any ranking system of countries who compete at the Olympic Games, it keeps a medal count. It ranks the participating countries by the number of gold medals won, then considers the number of silver medals won and then the number of bronze medals won. If two countries tie for results, they are listed in alphabetical order. The IOC's charter states that the Olympic Games is a competition among individual athletes and teams rather than countries. Other forms of ranking which differ from the gold-first ranking include a per-capita ranking (where the number of medals is divided by the population of the country); while the weighted-ranking system awards the most points for gold medal wins, with less for silver medals and less still for bronze medals won.

BOLD WORDS

Page 19

• Write the meaning of each word as found in a dictionary or online resource: *interferes*—meddles with, interrupts, disrupts; *focus*—concentrate, centre; *quest*—search, journey; *fruition*—attain something desired, reach a goal; *sacrifice*—actions to give up something in favour of something else; *agonising*—extremely painful, tortuous; *anguished*—suffering, distressed; *ultimate*—final aim or object.

ANSWERS

Page 20

1. an Olympic gold medal

2. 'One step at a time. Day after day. Year after year. Long days of training as the finish line appears.'

3. (a) 'Up with the dawn'.

   (b) 'Living for sport'

4. 'Toughen the body. Focus the mind.'

5. (a) 'Follow the coach. Practise the skills.'

   (b) 'Local, national, international competitions.'

   (c) 'The struggle, the cost, the sacrifice is expected.'

6. family and friends

7. 'agonising pain', 'crushing defeat', 'anguished teammates'

8. verse six

Page 21

1. (a) (i) Answers should indicate that there are many more people in both the USA and United Kingdom as compared to Ireland.

      (ii) Answers should indicate that because there are more people in the USA and UK, they are likely to have a greater chance of winning medals.

   (b) USA: 56 to 174; UK: 11 to 47; Ireland: 0 to 5

   (c) USA: 1 to 3; UK: 4 to 36; Ireland: 16 to 64 (or no ranking)

2.–3. Teacher check

ADDITIONAL ACTIVITIES

• Many athletes have their own websites, blogs or social networking webpages which describe their training and competition performances. Find one for your favourite Olympic or elite athlete and follow his/her progress.

• Discuss how elite athletes must give up many normal activities such as socialising with friends, going to the cinema or parties etc. in order to concentrate on their training.

What does it take to become an Olympian? – 1

Read the poem.

1. I dream of gold. It's my ultimate goal.
   To be the best in the world burns deep in my soul.
   One step at a time. Day after day. Year after year.
   Long days of training as the finish line appears.

2. Up with the dawn. Living for sport.
   Nothing **interferes** with the prize that is sought.
   Toughen the body. **Focus** the mind.
   Believe in myself and the strength I can find.

3. Follow the coach. Practise the skills.
   Improve each time for the love and the thrills.
   Local, national, international competitions;
   To do well in all brings the **quest** to **fruition**.

4. The struggle, the cost, the **sacrifice** is expected.
   Family and friends keep the fire attended.
   The ultimate test for body and mind.
   After all this time, at the end of the line, what prize will I find?

5. Through **agonising** pain and crushing defeat,
   All the **anguished** teammates I've managed to beat.
   These thoughts echo clearly and bring comfort and relief.
   You made it so far. There's no reason for grief.

6. You've been chosen for the team.
   You've achieved one part of your dream.
   For yourself and your country, you can only do your best.
   This alone is the **ultimate** test.

Fast fact: Olympian Tom Kiely paid his own fare to travel to the 1904 Summer Olympics in St Louis USA, despite being offered assistance from the United Kingdom and the United States. He wanted to compete for Ireland. He won a gold medal in the decathlon (then known as the 'All-Around Championship', which was ten events on the one day). His gold medal win was originally credited to the United Kingdom. However, many Olympic historians assign his win to Ireland.

Complete the following using the poem on page 19.

1. What is the gold the athlete dreams of?

_____

2. Which lines of the poem tell you that it takes a long time and a lot of training for an athlete to be selected for an Olympic team? Copy them below.

_____

_____

_____

3. Which phrases in verse 2 tell you that:

(a) athletes train early in the day?

_____

(b) athletes must love the sport they compete in?

_____

4. Athletes must be mentally and physically tough to succeed in their chosen sport. Which line in verse 2 states this?

_____

_____

5. Write the lines or words in verses 3 and 4 of the poem that state athletes:

(a) need to learn specific skills in their chosen sport from an expert to reach the Olympic level.

_____

_____

(b) must compete in many levels of competition to reach the Olympic level.

_____

_____

(c) need money to pay for gear and equipment, coaching and travel to sporting competitions.

_____

_____

6. In verse 4, which groups of people are very important in providing moral support for an elite athlete?

_____

7. The first two lines of verse 5 tell about some of the difficulties of being an elite athlete. What are three of these?

_____

_____

8. Which verse tells that it is an extremely great honour and amazing achievement to be chosen as a representative of your own country for an Olympic sport?

_____

_____

1. Compare the total number of Olympic medals won by the three countries at different Olympic Games. The table shows each country's medal tally and ranking at each Summer Olympics since 1924. The current population of each country is also listed.

	Number of medals won (Ranking at Games)		
	USA	**United Kingdom**	**Ireland**
Pop.	313 232 044	62 698 362	4 670 976
1924	99 (1)	34 (4)	0
1928	56 (1)	20 (11)	1 (24)
1932	103 (1)	16 (8)	2 (16)
1936	56 (2)	14 (10)	Did not compete
1948	84 (1)	23 (12)	0
1952	76 (1)	11 (18)	1 (34)
1956	74 (2)	24 (8)	5 (21)
1960	71 (2)	20 (12)	0
1964	90 (1)	18 (10)	1 (35)
1968	107 (1)	13 (10)	0
1972	94 (2)	18 (12)	0
1976	94 (3)	13 (13)	0
1980	Did not compete	21 (9)	2 (31)
1984	174 (1)	37 (11)	1 (33)
1988	94 (3)	24 (12)	0
1992	108 (2)	20 (13)	2 (32)
1996	101 (1)	15 (36)	4 (28)
2000	97 (1)	28 (10)	1 (64)
2004	103 (1)	31 (10)	0
2008	110 (2)	47 (4)	3 (61)

(a) (i) How do the populations of the USA and United Kingdom compare to that of Ireland?

(ii) What effect might this have on the quantity of medals won by each nation?

(b) Write the range of medal tallies for each country from least to most won.

- USA: ☐ to ☐

- United Kingdom: ☐ to ☐

- Ireland: ☐ to ☐

(c) Write the rankings from best to worst for each country.

- USA: ☐ to ☐

- United Kingdom: ☐ to ☐

- Ireland: ☐ to ☐

2. Use the following headings to research and complete your own table about Ireland's medal results in Olympic Games since 1924: Games (Year), Medal won, Name of athlete, Sport, Event.

The following websites may assist you with your research:

<http://www.olympicsport.ie/about/3022-oci-history.html>.

<http://www.databaseolympics.com/country/countrypage.htm?cty=IRL>

3. With a partner, decide which sports Ireland traditionally does well in at the Olympic Games, and find out which sports Ireland could do well in at the London Games.

ireland at other olympic competitions

objective

- Reads and completes activities about Ireland's participation in other Olympic competitions.

teacher information

- The idea to hold a Youth Olympic Games was suggested by Johann Rosenzopf, the Austrian IOC delegate, in 1998. It was conceived in response to growing concerns about increased childhood obesity, decreased youth participation in sporting activities in developing countries, and a reduction in sporting and physical activities in schools.

- The Youth Olympic Games follow a similar format to the Olympic Games: there is a Summer and Winter Games held every four years. However, there are some differences. The age groupings are: 14–15 years, 16–17 years and 17–18 years. The sports are similar to the Olympic Games but there are a limited number of disciplines and events as organisers do not want host cities to have to build costly venues or transport systems. It is believed this will allow smaller cities to have the opportunity to host a Youth Olympic Games. The first Youth Winter Olympic Games will be held from 13 to 22 January 2012 at Innsbruck, Austria. About 1100 athletes from over 60 nations will compete. Visit <http://www.innsbruck2012.com/en> to find information.

- The best result for Ireland at the Winter Olympic Games was obtained by Clifton Wrottesley who ranked 4th in skeleton in 2002.

- Visit <http://www.olympicsport.ie/> to find out more about Ireland at the Youth Olympic Games.

bold words

- Research to find out what the sports are and what they entail, then write a few sentences which briefly explain them.

answers

1. Games, Youth, European, Olympic
2. Winter, skeleton
3. boxing, sailing
4. Innsbruck
5. EYOF
6. athletics

A	S	I	H	C	T	B	S	N	N	H	W
S	R	C	U	T	O	G	O	I	A	O	I
V	A	P	I	X	U	T	F	D	E	L	N
E	J	I	I	T	E	O	W	Q	P	Y	T
Y	E	N	L	L	E	X	Y	F	O	M	E
O	G	K	E	I	N	L	L	E	R	P	R
F	D	K	A	M	N	Z	H	M	U	I	G
L	S	E	M	A	G	G	J	T	E	C	B
K	C	U	R	B	S	N	N	I	A	K	C

additional activities

- Use the information in the text to write clues for a crossword for a partner to complete. Use an online free crossword maker if desired.

- Follow the results of the Irish athletes at the inaugural Winter Youth Games in Innsbruck between 13–22 January 2012.

- Divide a large sheet of art paper into six sections. Label each with a Summer or Winter Olympic competition from the text, then use sketches to depict the different sports Ireland competes in at each.

Ireland at other Olympic competitions

Ireland participates in many international sporting competitions besides the Summer Olympic Games. These include the Winter Olympic Games, the Summer and Winter Youth Olympics, and the Summer and Winter European Youth Olympic Festivals (EYOF).

Excepting 1994, a team has represented Ireland at the Winter Olympic Games since 1992. Teams and individuals have competed in **bobsleigh**, alpine and cross-country skiing and **skeleton** events. For nearly each successive Games, more competitors have entered an increasing number of sports.

At the first Summer Youth Olympic Games in Singapore in 2010, an Irish boxer, Ryan Burnett, won a gold medal. Twenty-five athletes competed in eight sports—athletics, boxing, hockey, **modern pentathlon**, rowing, sailing, tennis and **triathlon**.

The first Winter Youth Olympic Games will be held in Innsbruck, Austria in 2012. Seven sports will be contested by athletes aged between 14 and 18 years.

The European Youth Olympic Festivals are held biennially for young athletes from 48 countries. Summer and winter versions are held at different venues in the same year. In 2009, at the Summer Festival, Ireland won one gold, three silver and three bronze medals. These were in the sports of swimming and athletics. At the 2011 Summer Festival, Ireland won two gold, one silver and four bronze medals.

A	S	I	H	C	T	B	S	N	N	H	W
S	R	C	U	T	O	G	O	I	A	O	I
V	A	P	I	X	U	T	F	D	E	L	N
E	J	I	I	T	E	O	W	Q	P	Y	T
Y	E	N	L	L	E	X	Y	F	O	M	E
O	G	K	E	I	N	L	L	E	R	P	R
F	D	K	A	M	N	Z	H	M	U	I	G
L	S	E	M	A	G	G	J	T	E	C	B
K	C	U	R	B	S	N	N	I	A	K	C

Find the answers in the word search.

1. The six different Olympic competitions in which Ireland participates are the Summer Olympic Games, the Winter Olympic _____, the Summer and Winter _____ Olympics, and the Summer and Winter _____ Youth _____ Festivals.

2. Irish teams and individual athletes have competed at the _____ Olympic Games since 1992 in bobsleigh, alpine and cross-country skiing, and _____.

3. Ryan Burnett won a gold medal in _____ at the 2010 Summer Youth Olympic Games. Other sports Irish athletes competed in included triathlon, tennis, athletics, hockey, _____, modern pentathlon and rowing.

4. The venue for the first Winter Youth Olympic Games is _____.

5. The abbreviation for the European Youth Olympic Festival is _____.

6. Ireland won medals at the 2009 European Youth Summer Olympic Festival in the sports of swimming and _____.

past irish olympians

objective

• Reads information and completes an activity about past Irish Olympians.

teacher information

• Bob Tisdall displayed true sportsmanship throughout his sporting career. At Cambridge, he allowed his teammate, Ted Cawston, to take his place in the 220 yard low hurdles so that Cawston would qualify to win his sporting 'blues' (an honour given to sportsmen and women at the University of Cambridge). After his gold medal win, Tisdall went immediately to the throwing area to encourage his friend and teammate Dr Pat O'Callaghan as he won an Irish gold medal too with his last throw of the competition.

• Later the rules for gaining a world record in hurdling were changed because of Bob Tisdall's incident in his gold medal-winning race.

• Ron Delany remained the only Irish gold medal-winning Olympic champion for 36 years until Michael Carruth won a gold medal in boxing at the 1992 Barcelona Olympic Games.

• In her competition days, Sonia O'Sullivan was considered one of the best middle-distance runners in the world.

bold words

Page 25

• Change one letter in each word to spell a new word. Suitable answers may include: born/burn, won/win/ton, long/lone/lung, write/wrote, compete/compute, part/port, time/tome, team/tear, last/lost/list/past, ever/even, gold/golf/gild, rules/roles, age/ate/ale/ape.

Page 26

• Write the bold words in one paragraph of text, using them in a non-sporting context which gives the meaning of each word. The text can be humorous and/or fantastical.

Page 27

• Write rhyming words for each bold word, then use as many of the pairs as possible to write a poem relating to sport.

answers

Page 25

1. Teacher check
2. He was still able to jog the 500 metres required in the Sydney 2000 Olympic Games torch relay.
3. Teacher check

Page 26

1. Teacher check
2. (a) 6/3/1935 (b) 3 (c) 1954
   (d) 1956 (e) 1956 (f) 1958
   (g) 6th (h) 4 (i) 3
   (j) 40

Page 27

1. (a) title   (b) seventeen
   (c) scholarship   (d) distances
   (e) marathon   (f) record
   (g) team   (h) international
   (i) third   (j) 5000 m
   (k) Sydney   (l) completed
   (m) champion   (n) London
   (o) Women's   (p) citizen
   (q) 2008   (r) manager
   (s) Championships (t) Scotland
2. Teacher check

additional activities

• Visit <http://www.sceala.com/phpBB2/irish-forums-841.html> to read more incidents in the amazing sporting career and life of Bob Tisdall.

• Visit <http://www.youtube.com/watch?v=cksaqL6kPnY> to view highlights of Sonia O'Sullivan's career.

Past Irish Olympians – 1

Robert (Bob) Tisdall was an Irish athlete who was born in Ceylon (now Sri Lanka) on 16 May 1907.

Raised in Nenagh, County Tipperary, Tisdall **won** the Public Schools 402 metres running race. At Cambridge University, he won a record four events—the 402 metres, the 110 metres hurdles, the **long** jump and the shot-put—while competing against Oxford University.

Tisdall decided to **write** to the President of the Irish Olympic Council for permission to **compete** as **part** of the 1932 Irish Olympic team in Los Angeles. He wanted to race in the 400 m hurdles event. He was invited to compete in an Olympic trial at Croke Park in Dublin, but failed to qualify the first **time** he tried. On his second attempt, he won the 402 metres hurdles at the Irish Championships and qualified for the Irish Olympic **team**.

At the 1932 Los Angeles Olympic Games he qualified for the the 400 m hurdles final. During the race, he was so far ahead that he thought that the other competitors might have fallen over. The break in concentration caused him to stumble over the **last** hurdle. Nevertheless, he finished in 51.7 seconds, breaking the world record and winning a gold medal. He was the second Irishman to **ever** win a **gold** medal. However, according to the **rules** at the time, because he knocked over the final hurdle, his time was not recorded as a world record.

In 2000, at the **age** of 93, he jogged 500 metres of the Torch Relay for the Sydney Olympic Games. At the time of his death in 2004, he was the oldest living track and field Olympic gold medallist.

1. What qualities or actions of Bob Tisdall tell you that he was a true Olympian?

2. Which event tells you that he continued his love of sport throughout his lifetime?

3. On the back of the worksheet, write some other interesting facts about Bob Tisdall's life that you have gathered by your own research.

Fast fact: Bob Tisdall is thought to have trained for competition by running around rows of trees in an orchard and hurdling over sheep grazing in the countryside.

Past Irish Olympians – 2

1. Read the table of information about Ron Delany, middle distance runner.

Date and place of birth	6 March 1935, Arklow, County Wicklow
Education	• Catholic University School, Dublin • Villanova University, Philadelphia, USA
Sporting career and highlights	• Won 3 National College Athletic Association **titles** • Reached 800 m final at 1954 European Championships, Bern, Switzerland • 1956 became the 7th runner to run a mile in less than 4 minutes • Qualified for Irish team to attend 1956 Melbourne Olympic Games; ran 1500 m finals in record time and won the gold medal; became the first Irishman to win an Olympic title in athletics since Bob Tisdall in 1932 • 1958 European **Championships**: won bronze medal in 1500 m event • 1960 Rome Olympic Games: finished 6th in 800 m quarter-final • Won 4 successive **Amateur** Athletic Union (AAU) titles in the 1 mile race • Broke world indoor mile record 3 times
Other achievements	Awarded Honorary Doctorate of Laws degree by University College, Dublin, in 2006
Greatest achievements	• Only Irish athlete to win an Olympic gold medal in a running event • Ran 40 **consecutive** track races without loss

2. Write numerals or numerical words or phrases to complete the answers.

(a) Date, month and year of birth. _____

(b) Number of national titles won at college. _____

(c) Year of first international championship. _____

(d) Year became only the 7th runner to conquer the 4-minute mile. _____

(e) Year of Olympic gold medal win in Melbourne. _____

(f) Year of bronze medal win at European Championships. _____

(g) Finishing position in 800 m quarter-final. _____

(h) Number of AAU titles won. _____

(i) Number of times broke world indoor mile record. _____

(j) Number of consecutive wins. _____

Past Irish Olympians – 3

1. Complete the cloze using the words below.

scholarship	marathon	distances	citizen
international	title	record	team
completed	London	third	Sydney
seventeen	manager	Women's	2008
Championships	Scotland	champion	5000 m

Sonia O'Sullivan was born in Cobh, County Cork, in 1969.

Sonia loved to run even as a child, and won her **first** championship _____ a

at the Irish Cross-Country Championships when she was _____ b years

old. She then **gained** an athletics _____ c for Villanova University in the

USA. Her competition _____ d have included the 1500 m, 3000 m,

5000 m, 10 000 m, 4 km, 8 km and _____ e (about 42 km). Her favourite

distance is the 5000 m. She has an **impressive** _____ f of individual and

_____ g results in various _____ h competitions from

1991 to 2002. This includes at **least** eight wins, six second-places and two

_____ i –places. Her most impressive result was a silver **medal** in the

_____ j race at the _____ k 2000 Olympic Games. At the Athens

2004 Olympic Games' 5000 m final, she _____ l the race, despite illness,

in front of a rousing crowd, thereby showing the qualities of a **true** _____ m.

In 2005, Sonia finished both the _____ n Marathon (in eighth **place**) and

the Dublin Women's Mini Marathon. Her record winning time in the Dublin _____ o

Mini Marathon has yet to be **beaten**. In 2006, she became a **dual** _____ p of

Ireland and Australia and now **lives** part of the year in each location.

In _____ q, she was appointed team _____ r of the Australian team for

the 2008 International Association of Athletics Federations (IAAF) World Cross-Country

_____ s in Edinburgh, _____ t.

2. Reread the completed cloze.

> ***Fast fact:*** Sonia O'Sullivan is the 2012 Irish Olympic team's Chef de Mission.

current irish olympic hopefuls

objective

- Reads information and completes an activity about three Irish athletes who hope to be successful at the 2012 Olympic Games.

teacher information

- Paul Hession was studying medicine at the National University of Dublin until he took time off to concentrate on his athletics training.

bold words

Page 29

- Compile a list of unusual 'colour' words (such as 'puce', 'indigo', 'violet' etc.) to add to 'silver' and 'bronze', then add other words to 'first' to write a list of ordinal numbers. Incorporate some more complicated examples, such as 'thirty-fifth' or 'twenty-eighth'.

Page 30

- Arrange the words in alphabetical order. Answers should be: advantage, child, competitions, conditions, equestrian, impressive, international, mount, partnership, personality, shortlisted, trains. If possible, find other words to alphabeticise for the letters in the alphabet not included in the list. For example, 'b', 'd', 'f', 'g', 'h'.

answers

Page 29

1. Teacher check

2. Answers will be similar to those given:

DOWN

1. (KOREA) Country where Paul won silver at World University Games.

3. (FIRST) In 1998, Paul completed and won his _____ Irish title./Paul was the _____ Irishman to qualify for the 200 m sprint in the European Athletics Championships in Barcelona.

4. (SILVER) Medal won in 200 m final at Stuttgart 2008 World Athletics Final.

ACROSS

2. (BRONZE) Medal won in 200 m sprint at 2005 World University Games in Turkey.

5. (QUALIFIED) _____ for the Beijing 2008 and London 2012 Olympic Games.

7. (FIFTEEN) Age at which he entered and won his first Irish title.

8. (BEIJING) Location of 2008 Olympic Games at which Paul competed.

Page 30

1. Pupils should choose from the Calgary Atco Power Stakes, the London Hickstead Speed Derby, the Grand Prix, the Xerox Cup, the Gentleman's Championship, the Nations Cup, the Hoys Classic, the Newcomers' Championship, the British Open Championships, and the Horse and Hound Foxhunter.

2. Some horses may be better suited to specific courses or conditions; one may be needed as backup in case of injury to another.

3. Answers will vary but should indicate that because of his background he grew up being familiar with equestrian sports and it was natural to begin competing in equestrian events at an early age.

Page 31

ACROSS 2. gold 4. amateur 6. Elite 10. welterweight 11. Six 12. boys

DOWN 1. youth 3. national 5. Best 7. lightweight 8. Mexico 9. First

additional activities

- Find out more about Paul Hession on his web page <http://www.paulhession.co/>. See a gallery of photos, and read his blog, biography and media releases.

- Follow Billy Twomey's progress and find information about him on his website <http://www.billytwomey.com/>.

Current Irish Olympic hopefuls – 1

1. Read the time line of information about Paul Hession, a sprinter who specialises in the 60 m, 100 m and 200 m sprint, both indoors and on the track.

1983	Born 27 January in Athenry, County Galway
1998	Competed in, and won, his first Irish title
2002	Competed in the World Junior Championships and the European Championships
2003	• Finished fifth at the European Under 23 Championships • Won a **silver** medal at the World University Games in Daegu, Korea
2004	Narrowly missed qualifying for the Athens Olympic Games by 0.02 seconds
2005	Won a **bronze** medal in the 200 m sprint at the World University Games in Izmir, Turkey
2007	Broke Irish national records in the 100 m and 200 m
2008	• Qualified for the Beijing 2008 Olympic Games but failed to reach the finals when he finished fifth in a semi-final heat. (Only the **first** four placegetters enter the finals!) His final world overall ranking was 10th. • Won a silver medal in the 200 m sprint at the World Athletics Final in Stuttgart, Germany • Named 'Athlete of the Year' by the Athletic Association of Ireland
2009	Finished sixth in semi-final at World Championships in Berlin, Germany
2010	• Became the first Irishman to qualify for the 200 m in the European Athletics Championships in Barcelona, Spain • Finished sixth in final at European Championships
2011	• Qualified for the 2012 Olympic Games when he won the 200 m event at the Senior Track and Field Championships in Dublin

2. On the back of this worksheet:

(a) write DOWN or ACROSS and the numbers for the answers; then

(b) write a clue for each answer in the crossword.

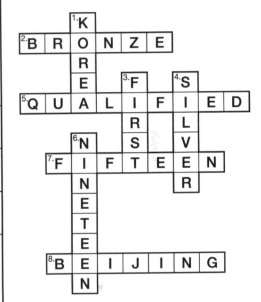

IRELAND

Fast fact: Paul has been called by some 'The fastest man in Ireland'.

Current Irish Olympic hopefuls – 2

Billy Twomey is an **equestrian** who specialises in show jumping as an individual and as a member of Irish team events. Currently he is ranked 11th in the world and first in Ireland.

Riding has been a large part of Billy Twomey's life since he was a **child**. His mother runs a riding school, his aunt is a well-known show jumping **personality**, and his uncle **trains** horses for the national hunt (races where horses are required to jump obstacles such as fences or hurdles). He began competing at the age of six.

From 2000 to 2011, Twomey has had an **impressive** run of results in national and **international** competitions. He was **shortlisted** for the Irish equestrian team to compete at the Sydney Olympic Games. He has won and gained places in competitions such as the Calgary Atco Power Stakes in Canada, the London Hickstead Speed Derby, the Grand Prix (the highest level of competition), the Xerox Cup, the Gentleman's Championship, the Nations Cup, the Hoys Classic, the Newcomers' Championship, the British Open Championships, and the Horse and Hound Foxhunter.

The equestrian sport of show jumping is a **partnership** between the rider and his or her horse. Having the best **mount** possible gives the rider an **advantage** in competition. Billy's mounts have been Luidam, Pikap, Je T'aime Flamenco, Tinka's Serenade and Romanov II. Riders can change horses for competitions depending on the course or **conditions**. Some riders own and ride their own horses, while others ride horses owned by others. Twomey's horses have won and placed in the Speed Horse of the Year and Leading Show Jumper of the Year **competitions**.

1. Name at least five national or international equestrian competitions.

_____

_____

_____

2. Why is it necessary to have more than one mount for competitions?

_____

_____

3. What aspect of Billy's family background do you think had an influence on his choice of career?

_____

_____

Fast fact: In 2008, Twomey suffered a broken leg, broken ribs and head injuries in a riding accident. Pikap, the mount he was hoping to ride at the Olympics, was killed and Twomey was unable to ride for six months.

Current Irish Olympic hopefuls – 3

Ray Moylette is an amateur boxer from Islandeady, County Mayo, who has competed in the lightweight (57–60 kg) and light welterweight (60–64 kg) divisions.

Ray has been boxing since the age of six and has won national titles in boys and youth divisions, including, in 2007, the Cadet and Youth (Under 19) divisions. He was also awarded a Best Boxer of the Championships title. In 2008, he won a gold medal at the World Youth Amateur Boxing Championships in Mexico. He was the first Irish boxer to accomplish this feat. In 2010, Ray was the Irish Elite champion, and, in 2011, he won a gold medal in the light welterweight division at the European Amateur Boxing Championships in Turkey.

Use the information in the text and the clues to find answers to complete the crossword.

Across

2. Medal won in Mexico.

4. Not professional.

6. Was Irish ____ champion in 2010.

10. A heavier boxing weight division.

11. Age Ray began boxing.

12. Very young males.

Down

1. Under 19.

3. Not international.

5. Won ____ Boxer of the Championships title in 2007.

7. A lighter weight division of boxing.

8. Country where gold medal won at World Youth Amateur Boxing Championships in 2008.

9. ____ Irish boxer to win a gold medal at the World Youth Amateur Boxing Championships in Mexico.

Fast fact: After his gold medal win in Turkey at the European Amateur Boxing Championships, Ray showed his elation by doing a handstand in the ring.

Olympic Council
of Ireland

irish code of ethics for sport

objective

- Reads information and completes an activity relating to the Irish Sports Council Code of Ethics.

teacher information

- Visit <http://www.irishsportscouncil.ie/Participation/Code_of_Ethics/> to download a copy of the Code of Ethics manual.

- The Irish Code of Ethics was introduced to try to ensure that children's 'early experiences of sport are positive and enjoyable, irrespective of their ability, gender, social class, race, etc.' (Refer to <http://www.irishsportscouncil.ie/Participation/Code_of_Ethics/>.)

- The Code aims to eradicate all forms of bullying by leaders, parents and other players from any sport in which a child participates.

bold words

- Use a dictionary to find the meaning of each bold word, then write a synonym and an antonym for each (if possible). Use the table as a guideline for examples of answers. Pupils should try to write a synonym which could be substituted for the word in the text without changing the meaning.

answers

- All boxes should be ticked as they are intended to give pupils examples of the types of actions that are expected from people who follow the Code of Ethics.

additional activities

- Discuss other actions which would fit the Code of Ethics for each group and those that would not.

- Ask the pupils to give examples of scenarios where they have observed players, parents or leaders displaying (or not displaying) actions which follow the Code.

Bold words possible answers			
Word	Meaning	Synonym	Antonym
guidelines	general instructions	instructions; rules	—
exhibit	display, expose, show	show, display	hide, conceal
controlled	restrained, commanded, dominated	ruled	uncontrolled
ethics	rules of conduct, a system of moral principles	morals, rules	—
organisations	bodies of people organised for some end or work	groups	individuals
friendly	kind, favourably disposed; inclined to approve, help, or support	kind, nice, supportive	unsupportive
code	a system of rules and regulations	rules	—
skills	the ability that comes from knowledge, practice, aptitude	practices	theories
leaders	people who lead, the head of an organisation	heads, organisers	followers
expected	assumed, anticipated	supposed to, should	unexpected
respect	esteem, regard	esteem	disrespect
consideration	thoughtful or sympathetic regard or respect; thoughtfulness for others	thoughtfulness	thoughtlessness

Irish Code of Ethics for Sport

A code of ethics is a set of **guidelines** for members of a particular group. It states the behaviours the members should **exhibit**. Many organisations are **controlled** by a code of **ethics**.

The Irish Sports Council and the Sports Council of Northern Ireland published a Code of Ethics for Children's Sport in 2000 for all sporting groups to follow. The Code of Ethics tries to get sporting clubs and **organisations** to make sport safe, fun, **friendly** and fair for all children so they will keep playing and enjoying sport into adulthood. The **code** states that children should learn new **skills** and make friends while enjoying sport in the spirit of fair play. For this to happen, the **leaders** of sporting clubs and groups, as well as parents, are **expected** to behave in ways that follow the Code of Ethics. All parties must treat each other with **respect** and **consideration**. (This includes players of an opposing team.)

For each group below, tick the actions which demonstrate the Code of Ethics guidelines then write examples of your own.

Parents should ...	Leaders should ...	Players should ...
• not embarrass, belittle or abuse their own or other children, other parents or officials ☐	• treat all players with respect and dignity ☐	• be good losers and winners ☐
• behave responsibly ☐	• listen to players ☐	• compete at a level where they feel comfortable ☐
• applaud good play on both sides ☐	• allow all players to participate equally ☐	• follow the rules of the team and sport ☐
• encourage their children to play by the rules ☐	• be suitably qualified ☐	• treat all leaders and players with respect
• act as a role model for their children ☐	• place the safety of the children and the dignity of the sport first ☐	• be allowed to participate on an equal basis ☐
•	• create a positive atmosphere to learn new skills ☐	•
	•	

OLYMPIC COUNCIL OF IRELAND

emblems of the 2012 games

objectives

- Finds information on the internet about the Olympic and Paralympic emblems.

- Conducts a simple survey to determine preferred emblem.

teacher information

- A new emblem is designed for each Olympic Games. Incorporating the Olympic rings, the design of the emblem is often a statement of the culture of the host city and nation.

- The 2012 emblem was designed to inspire young people across the globe to feel the Olympic spirit and strive to achieve their best in all personal goals. The organisers of the London Games hope that the emblem will serve to remind people of the Olympic values.

- The decision to use the same emblem for the Olympic and Paralympic Games was deliberate as the Paralympic movement was founded in Britain.

- The colouring of the London 2012 Paralympic Games emblem will not change but will incorporate the four colours allowed for the London Olympic Games emblem. The emblem includes the logo of the International Paralympic Committee in place of the five Olympic Rings. The words 'Paralympic Games' are written on the second 2 of 2012.

- The website <http://www.colourlovers.com/blog/2008/08/18/design-and-branding-trends-olympic-games/> shows the emblems of all the Summer Olympics from the first Olympiad in Athens in 1896 to the 30th Olympiad in London in 2012.

- The Olympic emblem is incorporated in the uniform of every Olympic competitor.

answers

1. Teacher check
2. (a) The five Olympic rings
   (b) Three curved 'ticks' or 'agitos' which are usually red, blue and green, but on the emblem are all white.
3. Teacher check

additional activities

- Create a timeline of Olympic emblems from Athens 1896 to Rio de Janeiro 2016. Display the timeline close to a world map. Use coloured wool and pins to match each emblem to its host city.

- Hold a competition to design an emblem for the class or school. Display all entries and select a time for people to vote for their favourite. Count votes and record as percentages. Display using different graphical representations.

Emblems of the 2012 Games

Emblems are symbols that represent things such as a place, an event or an organisation. They are used to create identity, raise awareness and advertise.

For each Olympiad, a unique emblem is designed. Since 1932, it has included the Olympic Rings. When the design is revealed to the public, it is an event and there is great excitement and media attention.

So what is the emblem for the Games of the XXX Olympiad in 2012? Log on to the official website *<http://www.london2012.com>* to see it.

1. In the box, draw and colour the emblem.

The graffiti–style design is based on the digits of 2012 and features the name of the host city, London, and the Olympic Rings within the digits. The same emblem will also be used for the Paralympic Games, which takes place two weeks after the Olympic Games finish. This is seen as a positive step in creating a bridge between the two international sporting carnivals. In spite of differences in the past, competing at the Olympics or the Paralympics is the pinnacle of every athlete's career.

The official colours of the emblem are blue, orange, green and pink, but the colours of sponsors of the Games can also be used (to advertise their involvement). At the Closing Ceremony of the Games, when London hands over control to Rio de Janeiro, the Union Jack flag of the United Kingdom will be used to colour the emblem.

The emblem is immediately recognisable as the symbol of the 2012 Olympics and the organisers of the Games hope it will appeal particularly to young people.

2. (a) Use the internet to research and find the feature on the 2012 Olympic emblem that has been changed for the Paralympic Games.

_____

_____

_____

(b) Draw the replacement feature in the box.

3. (a) Design an alternative emblem for the 2012 Olympic Games.

(b) Ask 12 people which emblem they prefer. How many votes did each emblem receive?

Emblem	Tally	Score
Official		
Yours		

mascots of the 2012 games

objectives

- Reads information about the origin of the names of the mascots.

- Finds information on the internet about the Olympic and Paralympic mascots.

teacher information

- Mascots have been a part of every Summer Olympics since Waldi the dachshund first appeared at the 1972 Montreal Olympics. The mascot for the Games of the XXX Olympiad is named Wenlock, while the mascot for the 2012 Paralympics is named Mandeville. The story is that both mascots were formed from the last two drops of British steel used in the construction of the Olympic Stadium.

- As they travel separately around the UK in the months preceding the Games, Wenlock and Mandeville aim to inspire people, especially the young, to strive to achieve their personal goals.

- On the official website <http://www.london2012.com/mascots> pupils can enjoy a number of activities, including watching animations of the two stories about the two mascots, *Out of a Rainbow* and *Adventures on a Rainbow*, both written by Michael Morpurgo.

- Discuss the design of Wenlock and Mandeville. What do the pupils like or dislike about them?

answers

Teacher check

additional activities

- Make a labelled display of each mascot playing different sports. Pictures for pupils to copy can be found on the mascot page of the official website <http://www.london2012.com/mascots>

- Pupils design, make and name an Olympic or Paralympic mascot. They describe and explain the role of any special features, materials from which it is made, or reasons for choice if a recognisable animal is used.

Mascots of the 2012 Games

The mascots of the 2012 Olympic and Paralympic Games are

Wenlock and Mandeville.

Visit the official website at *<http://www.london2012.com/mascots>* to see them.

1. Draw and colour the mascots in the boxes below.

Wenlock	**Mandeville**

As the athletes and the host city prepare for the Olympic and Paralympic Games, so the mascots, Wenlock and Mandeville, have been busy travelling around the United Kingdom, meeting people and learning all about the different sports.

The two mascots have a very special place in the history of the Modern Olympic and Paralympic Games.

Since the mid-19th century, the Olympian Society of Much Wenlock, a small town in the English countryside, has held an annual sports festival. In 1890, Baron Pierre de Coubertin visited Much Wenlock to watch the Games. They inspired him to form the International Olympic Committee, which worked together to establish the Modern Olympic Games.

After World War II, there were many soldiers at Stoke Mandeville Hospital in England who were adapting to the spinal injuries they had received during the war. On the day of the Opening Ceremony of the 1948 Olympic Games in London, Sir Ludwig Guttman organised a sports competition at the hospital for these soldiers. From these games, the Paralympic Games were born.

2. Using information from the website, describe the features of each mascot.

Wenlock	**Mandeville**

pictograms of the 2012 games

objectives

- Reads information about the London Games pictograms.
- Draws and describes the differences between pictograms of disciplines within the same sport.

teacher information

- Pictograms were first used at the 1948 Games in London but were not used regularly until the 1964 Games in Tokyo. Their purpose is to impart information to visitors and competitors from different countries who do not speak the language of the host nation. General information pictograms are used in addition to sport pictograms, helping people navigate their way through unfamiliar cities. Pictograms have proved to be invaluable at all Olympic Games. The website <http://olympic-museum.de/pictograms/Picto1964.htm> shows the pictograms used by each host city at all the Olympic Games since 1964.

- For the 2012 Games in London, there are 38 pictograms representing 26 sports and their individual disciplines. The sports which have more than one discipline, and therefore more than one pictogram, are:

  aquatics – *diving, swimming, synchronised swimming* and *water polo*

  canoeing – *slalom* and *sprint*

  cycling – *BMX, mountain bikes, road* and *track*

  equestrian – *dressage, eventing* and *show jumping*

  gymnastics – *artistic, rhythmic* and *trampoline.*

- For the 2012 Paralympic Games, there are 20 sports and 21 pictograms. Cycling has two disciplines, road and track. These can be viewed on the website <http://www.london2012.com/paralympic-sport>.

- Discuss the purpose of unique clothing and equipment used for different sports. Why do water polo players wear different coloured caps? (To distinguish team members.) Why do synchronised swimmers wear nose clips? (To prevent water going up their noses.) Why don't divers wear goggles? (To prevent goggles damaging eyes when entering water at speed.) What are the main pieces of equipment required for archery? (Bow, arrows, quiver, guards, target.) In weightlifting, why are weights put on both ends of the barbell and not just one? (To balance the barbell.)

answers

1. As it is an international event, many different languages will be spoken but everyone can understand the messages conveyed by pictograms.

2. (a) *Canoe:*

   slalom – *The canoeist sits within the enclosed canoe, using a paddle with a blade at each end. Hanging poles for him/her to navigate through are included.*

   sprint – *The canoeist kneels within the open canoe, using a paddle with a blade at one end only.*

   (b) *Cycling:*

   BMX – *Small open wheels and high handlebars with cyclist standing on pedals while wearing a full-face crash helmet.*

   track – *Standard-size disc wheels and low handlebars with cyclist leaning forward while wearing an aerodynamic teardrop-shaped helmet.*

3. Teacher check

additional activities

- Survey the most popular Olympic sports to watch. Use pictograms to represent each vote or group of votes.

- Pupils design pictograms for the 2012 Olympic sports. Pictogram designs can incorporate the movement, clothing and equipment of a sport.

Pictograms of the 2012 Games

Pictography is the art of using pictures to communicate meaning. If you have ever played the game 'Pictionary®', you will be very familiar with pictography. As no written words are used in a pictogram, its meaning can be understood across all languages. For this reason, pictograms are invaluable at the Olympic Games (where they have been used since the Tokyo Games in 1964) to communicate with visitors and athletes from many nations.

To view labelled pictograms for the 2012 Games, visit the webpage
<http://www.london2012.com/sport>.

In addition to the traditional silhouette version, there is a coloured dynamic version of the pictograms, inspired by the map of the London Underground.

To view these, visit the webpage at
<http://visualizedata.wordpress.com/2011/01/29/london-2012-olympic-pictograms/>.

The pictograms will appear on tickets, event programmes, signs directing people to sporting venues and on a range of Games merchandise.

1. At an event like the Olympic Games, what is the main advantage of pictograms?

_____

2. Draw the pictograms and describe the differences.

(a) Canoe – Slalom	Canoe – Sprint	Differences

(b) Cycling – BMX	Cycling –Track	Differences

3. Draw two 2012 Games pictograms. Ask a friend to identify them.

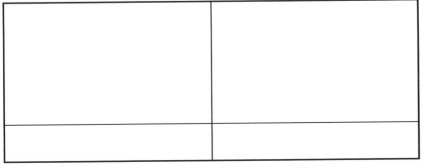

olympic games motto

objectives

- Shows understanding of the meaning of the Olympic motto.
- Considers how the meaning of the Olympic motto can be applied to all aspects of life.

teacher information

- The motto for all Olympic Games is 'Citius, Altius, Fortius', which means 'Swifter (Faster), Higher, Stronger'. This motto was originally used by a college principal in Paris who used it to inspire his pupils. The founder of the Modern Olympic Games, Baron de Coubertin, thought that it was the perfect motto to inspire athletes across the globe to reach the ultimate goal of becoming an Olympian and competing for an Olympic medal. The motto was first used at the Paris 1924 Olympic Games.

- Discuss 'Faster, Higher, Stronger' as a motto that can be used in everyday life by everybody—always strive to achieve your best in all areas of your life. Discuss examples of areas—such as school work, helping at home, treating people well—behaving well where the motto could be applied.

- Visit <http://janecky.com/olympics/creed.html> to read the Olympic Creed. Discuss how it relates to the Olympic Motto. To reach the Olympics, all athletes have had to constantly strive to improve their performances so that they are at the peak of their fitness. This has been their 'struggle', their 'fight'. In each event, only one person will win, will 'triumph', will 'conquer', and only three will have the glory of standing on the podium and receiving a medal. This does not mean that all the others have failed. In becoming Olympians, they have all succeeded; the medals are secondary for, without the intense competition of their rivals, how would anyone win?

answers

1. To compete at the Olympic Games to be an Olympian

2. (a) to be the best you can be

   (b) Answers will indicate: If all athletes strive to be the best they can be, the competition will be equal among competitors who have worked hard to reach their full potential.

3. Answers may include: … in all that you do, … in all areas of your life, … to make the most of your talents, … to make your life fulfilling.

additional activities

- For a chosen sport, discuss a training regime that would have to be adhered to if you wanted to follow the Olympic Motto. What sacrifices would you have to make? How difficult would it be to stick to? How much support would you need? How would it affect your school and family life? Do you think you could ever be dedicated enough to be an Olympian?

- Discuss a non-sporting area of your life. Explain how you could use the Olympic Motto to create a positive change in that area.

Olympic Games Motto

Every athlete dreams of competing at the Olympic Games; to be an Olympian and take part in the greatest sports carnival on Earth is the ultimate goal. Those who reach this goal are the ones who focus on the meaning of the Olympic Motto:

'Faster, Higher, Stronger'.

To compete at the Olympics, athletes must always strive to improve their personal performance and be the best they can possibly be. They must dedicate time and effort to achieve short-term goals until the ultimate goal is reached. This can mean hours of training before and after school or work, only eating healthy food and going to bed early. There can be no lie-ins, late nights or junk food for an aspiring Olympian! And as each short-term goal is reached, athletes are one step closer on their single-minded journey on the road to the Olympics.

Arriving at the Olympic Games well-prepared and in peak condition for competition, athletes have reached their ultimate goal. As they walk in the parade at the Opening Ceremony, they know they have completed the hardest part of the Olympic struggle and can look forward to the excitement of the carnival ahead.

Winning an Olympic medal is a prize to be cherished but it is not as important as taking part in the Games—for without other competitors, how can a winner be chosen? All Olympians have travelled on the same tough road, through highs and lows, to compete in the Games. They have all focused on the Olympic Motto:

'Faster, Higher, Stronger'.

1. What is the ultimate goal of every serious athlete?

_____

_____

2. (a) Tick the correct answer. 'Faster, Higher, Stronger' means:

- to be better than your competitors. ☐

- to be the best you can be. ☐

(b) Explain your choice of answer.

_____

_____

3. How would you extend the meaning of the Olympic Motto so that people can use it in their daily lives?

_____

_____

OLYMPIC COUNCIL OF IRELAND

olympic games torch and relay

objectives

- Locates image from given website to complete activity.
- Reads information about the Olympic Torch and Relay.

teacher information

- The Olympic Flame and the torches that carry it are special symbols of the Olympic Games. The lighting of the Olympic Flame involves a special traditional ceremony at the Temple of Hera in Olympia, Greece, where the Ancient Olympic Games were held. A parabolic (curved) mirror is used to focus the rays of the sun to a single point. The intense heat produced ignites the fuel in a torch and the Olympic Flame is lit. At an altar in the Ancient Olympic stadium, the first torchbearer's torch is lit from this flame. There follows a short relay around Greece before the Flame is handed to the host nation at another ceremony in Athens.

- The Flame remains alight on its journey to the host nation. In 2012, the Olympic Flame arrives in the UK in mid-May and begins a 70-day journey across the country, including a number of the smaller islands, where it spreads the message of 'peace, unity and friendship'. The Flame arrives in London at the end of July when the final torchbearer uses it to light the Olympic Cauldron at the Opening Ceremony. The Flame continues to burn for the duration of the Games and is not extinguished until the Closing Ceremony.

- During the Relay, it is the Flame that is the 'baton', passed between the torches of each torchbearer. Being a torchbearer is a great privilege. People from all walks of life who have been an inspiration to others can be nominated to become one. After their part of the relay, each torchbearer has the option to buy the torch as a souvenir of the occasion.

answers

1. Teacher check
2. (a) The Torch stands 800 mm tall and weighs 800 g.
   (b) 8000 embossed circles represent 8000 torchbearers
3. The torch is both tapered and light in weight.
4. Answers may be similar to:
   respect – *for culture and athletic ability;*
   friendship – *between rivals;*
   excellence – *athletes have worked hard to become Olympians in their chosen sport.*

additional activities

- From 18 May 2012, when the flame arrives in the UK from Greece, visit <*http://www.bbc.co.uk/news/uk-13391986*> and follow the relay to London. Display a large map of the UK and pin point each location.

- Discuss the meaning of 'inspirational'. Write a profile of someone who is a source of inspiration. This can be a famous person or someone close to you.

Olympic Games Torch and Relay

The lighting of the Olympic Torch at Olympia, the Torch Relay around the host country and its arrival at the Opening Ceremony of the Games are important parts of the Olympic Games tradition. They serve to invite people from all cultures to unite and enjoy the world's greatest sporting carnival.

For each Games, a new Torch is designed and mass-produced for the thousands of torchbearers who take part in the relay.

Visit the official website to see the torch:

<http://www.london2012.com/games/olympic-torch-relay/olympic-torch>.

The inspiration for the 2012 Torch's triangular design comes from the frequency of the number 3 in the history of the Games and the Olympic movement.

- respect, friendship, excellence ..... the Olympic values
- faster, higher, stronger .... the Olympic Motto
- peace, unity, friendship .... Torch Relay message
- 1908, 1948, 2012 .... the years London has hosted the Games
- sport, education, culture .... aspects of life combined at the 2012 Games

The Torch for the 2012 Games is 800 mm tall, tapering from top to bottom with a triangular cross-section. It is made from strengthened aluminium from which 8000 circles have been cut, one to represent each of the torchbearers. Through the circles, the internal burner which keeps the flame alive can be seen. These holes help to reduce the weight of the torch so that it can be carried by torchbearers as young as 12 years old. The total weight of the torch is 800 g.

Coming directly from Greece to the UK, the Relay starts at Land's End on the south-western tip of the UK. The route covers all regions of the UK, including some of its many islands.

The Flame will be carried among 8000 torches for 70 days before arriving at the Olympic Stadium to light the Olympic Cauldron at the Opening Ceremony.

1. From the official website, draw the 2012 Olympic Torch.

2. How are these numbers significant in the Torch's design?

(a) 800 _____

(b) 8000 _____

3. What are the two design features that make the Torch suitable for young torchbearers?

_____

_____

4. Explain what you understand by the Olympic values:

respect. _____

friendship. _____

excellence. _____

OLYMPIC COUNCIL OF IRELAND

sustainability in 2012

objectives

- Solves clues to demonstrate appreciation of the 'Sustainable Games'.
- Researches one aspect of sustainability at the 2012 Games.

teacher information

- When making the bid to host the Olympic Games, London promised to present the world with 'the first sustainable Olympic and Paralympic Games'. In doing so, they hope to inspire change in the behaviours and attitudes of people across the globe in relation to how we are consuming resources and producing pollution. It is recognised that, collectively, we are consuming resources at a far greater rate than the planet can hope to regenerate them. If the lifestyles of all countries were similar to that of many First World nations, we would need the resources of three planet Earths to maintain our living standards.

- The 'Towards a one planet Olympics' sustainability plan explains how the organising committee have incorporated sustainability in all stages of development of the preparation for the Games and construction of Olympic Park. It also describes how the legacy of the Games will continue and benefit the people of London and the UK when the Games are over.

- It is also hoped that the 2012 Games will inspire greater participation in sport and greater respect for those with disabilities. It is hoped that the Games will encourage people to experience the benefits sports provide.

- 2012 could be seen to be an important year for the future health of the planet; the Earth Summit (the United Nations Conference on Sustainable Development) takes place in early June just prior to the Olympics. Its goal is to ensure political commitment to sustainable development.

- For the activity on page 47, pupils should focus on the relevant pages to complete the task and not try to read the whole document.

answers

Page 46

1. (a) renewable energy technologies
   (b) using existing sports facilities
   (c) transforming a neglected area
   (d) reducing greenhouse gas emissions
   (e) reusing resources
   (f) restoring natural habitats
   (g) promoting greater biodiversity
   (h) accessibility for everyone
   (i) creating job opportunities
   (j) promoting healthier lifestyles

2. Teacher check

Page 47

Teacher check

additional activities

- In groups, prepare a bid to host the 2020 Olympic Games, focusing on the aspects of sustainability identified by the London committee. Pupils vote for the best group.

- How might an area in your locality be improved to increase its biodiversity? Describe the area as it is now, what you would do to improve it, and how it would then benefit the wildlife and the community when the work is completed.

2012 Irish Olympic Team in London   44   www.prim-ed.com   Prim-Ed Publishing

Sustainability in 2012 – 1

An industrial part of the city of London that used to be very grey and neglected has been transformed by the development of Olympic Park.

Olympic Park is the biggest city park to be built in Europe for more than 150 years. It is the main site and focus of the 2012 Games, although many world-class sporting facilities already in existence in the UK will be used for some sports.

When the bid was made to host the event, the Olympics organising committee who built the Park had one major goal: for the Games to be remembered as the 'Sustainable Games'. To realise this ideal, they focused on five key points.

Climate change – To reduce greenhouse gas emissions, renewable energy technologies such as wind turbines, solar panels and biomass fuel power generators have been installed to provide electricity, heating, cooling and hot water needs across the site.

Waste – Existing resources have been reused wherever possible; for example, soil from the original site was washed and sieved to remove impurities so that it could be reused; items such as bricks, paving slabs and lampposts have been reused in the park.

Biodiversity – Existing wetlands and other natural habitats have been restored and new ones have been provided to ensure minimal disturbance to wildlife already established, and to promote greater biodiversity in the area. The organising committee hopes that with a focus on conserving and promoting biodiversity, the bond between sport and caring for the environment will be strengthened.

Inclusion of all people – Providing wheelchair-friendly facilities and links to public transport has made the park accessible to everyone. After the Games, new permanent job opportunities will be available at the different venues.

Healthy living – To inspire people to take up sport and to have more active, healthier lifestyles, all the sports facilities will be available for the public to enjoy when the Games are over.

Even when the 2012 Olympic and Paralympic Games are over, the people of London will still have a beautiful park and new sports facilities to enjoy. The Athletes' Village will be transformed to provide 2800 new homes. The Park will be re-named the Queen Elizabeth II Olympic Park in honour of the Queen's Diamond Jubilee, which will be celebrated in June 2012.

Use the text on page 45 to answer the questions.

1. Use each clue and add the missing consonants to complete each 'sustainability phrase'.

   (a) Inventions for reuseable power sources

   □ e □ e □ a □ □ e / e □ e □ □ □ / □ e □ □ □ o □ o □ i e □

   (b) Venues already in place

   u □ i □ □ / e □ i □ □ i □ □ / □ □ o □ □ □ / □ a □ i □ i □ i e □

   (c) Improving a forgotten place

   □ □ a □ □ □ o □ □ i □ □ / a / □ e □ □ e □ □ e □ / a □ e a

   (d) Decreasing possible atmosphere-warming substances

   □ e □ u □ i □ □ / □ □ e e □ □ o u □ e / □ a □ / e □ i □ □ i o □ □

   (e) Employing something again

   □ e u □ i □ □ / □ e □ o u □ □ e □

   (f) Reviving wildlife-occupied environments

   □ e □ □ o □ i □ □ / □ a □ u □ a □ / □ a □ i □ a □ □

   (g) Increasing flora and fauna

   □ □ o □ o □ i □ □ / □ □ e a □ e □ / □ i o □ i □ e □ □ i □ □

   (h) Able to be used by all

   a □ □ e □ □ i □ i □ i □ □ / □ o □ / e □ e □ □ o □ e

   (i) Making new employment possibilities

   □ □ e a □ i □ □ / □ o □ / o □ □ o □ □ u □ i □ i e □

   (j) Advertising how to live better

   □ □ o □ o □ i □ □ / □ e a □ □ □ □ i e □ / □ i □ e □ □ □ □ □ e □

2. Write a short magazine article in support of the 2012 'Sustainable Games'.

   _____

   _____

   _____

   _____

   _____

Sustainability in 2012 – 3

Choose one of the key sustainability points from the text on page 45 and research how the 2012 Olympic Games committee has tried to implement its ideals.

Refer to the *Towards a One Planet – 2012* sustainability plan that can be be found at *<http://www.london2012.com/documents/locog-publications/london-2012-sustainability-plan.pdf>.*

Sustainability point	
What the 2012 committee hoped to achieve	
What the 2012 committee has achieved	
How successful do you think the committee has been in achieving this goal?	
Do you believe the committee's efforts have been worthwhile? Explain your answer.	

OLYMPIC COUNCIL
OF IRELAND

olympic venues outside London

objective

- Reads and understands information about the venues outside London that will be used for the Olympics.

teacher information

- Football is the most watched sport around the world and particularly in Britain. There are five stadiums outside of London where Olympic football matches can be seen during the Games. There are three in England and one each in Scotland and Wales. These are all very large stadiums and will allow many Britons living outside of London to participate in the Games.

- There are two lakes not far from London being used for canoeing and rowing events. These first class facilities will cater particularly well for spectators.

- The other water sports facility is for sailing. It is located in a beautiful setting on the south coast, south-east of London. The ever-changing conditions there will make it a challenging course for sailors. Sailing is not an easily observed sport, so video images will be provided. Spectators will have the opportunity of watching dinghies, keelboats and windsurfing boards on a video screen.

- Mountain bike events will also be held south of London. There, spectators will be able to view some fast and furious riding from temporary grandstands and along the course. The venue, with its rocky paths and tricky climbs, was the first to be ready for the Games.

- Pupils can discuss the questions and write their answers on a sheet of paper or on the back of the worksheet.

answers

1. Answers will vary but may include:
   To enable more people and those living outside London to watch/Because football is very popular in Britain.

2. Events are competed too far away to be seen by spectators on the shore.

3. Eton Dorney has still, calm water and slalom canoes need white water and an obstacle course.

additional activities

- Pupils use an atlas to locate each of the venues outside London.

- Research the capacity of each of the five stadiums and the number of matches to be played in each to calculate the number of people who could watch an Olympic football match outside of London (approximately 2 770 000).

1. Hampden Park

There will be eight men's and women's football matches played near Glasgow, Scotland. The stadium has been upgraded at a cost of 70 million pounds.

2. St James' Park

Newcastle-upon-Tyne will be the venue for nine football matches, including men's and women's quarter-finals.

3. Old Trafford

The famous home of the Manchester United Football Club was opened in 1910. There will be 76 000 seats available for nine football matches including the men's and women's semi finals.

4. City of Coventry Stadium

Twelve football matches, including the women's bronze medal match, will be watched at this stadium, built in 2005.

5. Millennium Stadium

The first Olympic event will be held in this stadium on the banks of the River Taff in Cardiff, Wales, on 25 July. Eleven football matches, including two quarter-finals and the men's bronze medal game, will be played in front of 74 600 spectators.

6. Lee Valley White Water Centre

A large new lake with two longer and one shorter canoe slalom courses has been constructed, with obstacles and pumps to supply the white water.

Hampden Park
St James' Park
Old Trafford
City of Coventry Stadium
Lee Valley White Water Centre
Millennium Stadium
Eton Dorney
Hadleigh Farm
Weymouth and Portland

7. Eton Dorney

Rowing and canoe sprints will take place in eight lanes on Dorney Lake, 40 kilometres from London. It is in a nature conservation area. A new bridge has been built over the lake for vehicle and pedestrian traffic.

8. Hadleigh Farm

There is a new mountain bike course in the hilly grasslands around the 700-year-old ruin of Hadleigh Castle. Spectators can watch races from along the course.

9. Weymouth and Portland

This bay is sheltered from waves and currents, but not from the wind. Spectators will stand and watch the sailing events happening at sea on a big video screen.

1. Why do you think so many football matches will be played outside London?

2. Explain why spectators of the sailing competitions will need to watch events on a video screen.

3. Why can't the canoe slalom and the canoe sprint events both be held at Eton Dorney?

getting around London

objective

- Reads and researches information to complete an information chart about the different forms of transport available in London.

teacher information

- It is expected that many spectators from Europe will travel to London during the Games. Eurostar™ is the official international rail services provider of the Games. It is expected to bring about one million people to London via the rail tunnel under the English Channel. On this daily service linking with the Olympic Javelin™ train, people will be able to travel from Brussels to Olympic Park in less than two hours.

- The high-speed Olympic Javelin™ has been supplied by Japan. It has been described as the 'jewel in the crown' of the transport plans for the Games. This high speed train will travel from central London to Stratford International Station at Olympic Park in just seven minutes at a speed of 140 mph. A video about the introduction of this train can be viewed at: <http://news.bbc.co.uk/2/hi/uk_news/8170846.stm>

- The London Underground (or 'The Tube', as it is more commonly called) opened in 1863. It was the first underground railway constructed in the world, built in an effort to solve the city's traffic congestion. It carries more than 3 million people each day and has 270 stations. It is the world's second biggest underground rail service. The entrances to its underground stations are an integral part of London's landscape.

- There will be more than 8500 buses in use during the Games. London buses are fitted with a state-of-the-art iBus™ tracking facility so they can be located by mobile phone. There is a countdown system used which tells passengers how long they need to wait for a bus at one of the 19 500 bus stops. Almost all buses are wheelchair accessible. The first five New Buses should be in service for the Games. These double-decker buses have three entrances and two staircases for quicker boarding. They are hybrid electric and diesel buses and cut

carbon emissions by about 30% from present levels. London will also have some hydrogen buses, which produce very low carbon emissions.

- Although some of the iconic black London taxis have been replaced with different coloured ones and by a number of minicabs, the black ones still dominate the streets of London. The fact that London's cabs are represented by the light placed on the top of Wenlock, the Olympic Mascot's head, is an indication of their national significance.

- The River Thames water taxis will offer a more leisurely journey to Olympic Park, Horse Guards Parade, and North Greenwich Arena. There is a dedicated river entrance at Olympic Park.

answers

Teacher check

additional activities

- Research the history of the London Tube or another large underground rail system in one of the world's major cities and prepare an oral or written report.

- Make a word search using words from the text on page 51.

Getting around London

Moving millions of people daily around any of the world's largest cities is never easy, but moving an additional influx of visitors around an already busy city is particularly challenging. This is why the transport arrangements for huge events like the Olympics need very careful planning and organisation.

Before they put in their bid to host the Olympics, planners in London spent two years looking for the best ways of transporting people to Olympic Park and other venues around the city. Their plan really impressed the Olympic deciding committee and it was one of the reasons why London's bid to host this event was successful.

Not only did the organisers need to move people around the city, they also wanted to make the Games sustainable by not causing more pollution or wasting resources so they couldn't be used later. They decided to improve their already excellent public transport system; particularly the railways, the water buses on the famous River Thames, buses (including their famous red double-decker ones) and London's well-known black taxis and modern mini cabs. Free public transport would be included in tickets to events to discourage private cars and there wouldn't be any new car parks built at venues. To provide access to some venues, 75 kilometres of cycling and walking paths would be built at a cost of 10 million pounds.

Transport to Olympic Park is mainly supplied by rail. There are 10 separate railway lines going there. These include the new high-speed Javelin™ shuttle service linking to Eurostar™ (the train from Europe via a tunnel under the English Channel). Javelin™ is capable of transporting 25 000 people an hour with a train arriving every 15 seconds. The driverless Docklands Light Rail overground trains link to the airport.

The Tube, London's underground railway, has been improved and its capacity upgraded by 45 per cent. These improvements will be appreciated by the millions of London's commuters who will continue to use it long after the Games.

Use the information provided and further research to complete the table about some different forms of transport visitors can use during the Games.

Name/Type of transport	Interesting features

olympic park

objective

- Reads information about the primary Games venue, Olympic Park, and composes questions.

teacher information

- The Olympic Stadium, Aquatics Centre, Basketball Arena, BMX Track, Eton Manor, Handball Arena, Hockey Centre, Veledrome and Water Polo Arena are the new venues constructed for the Games in Olympic Park at Stratford City in eastern London.

- This former industrial area has been transformed for the Games. The new park will feature a garden area with markets, entertainment, cafes and shops in the south and a quieter public space in the north, where over 300 000 native plants have been planted. Thirty bridges have been constructed within the park to enable people to move around the venues and to enjoy the very pleasant environment.

- The Athletes' Village, with accommodation for 17 000 competitors and officials, is in this park. The purpose-built accommodation has state-of-the-art facilities and is linked to central London by the Olympic Javelin™ train (a journey that takes only seven minutes). After the Olympics, the Village will be an attractive housing area. This is part of the organising committee's commitment to a focus on sustainability.

- The International Broadcasting Centre and the Main Press Centre (IBC/MPC), located in the north-west corner of the park, will provide 24-hour facilities and will cater for about 20 000 broadcasters, journalists and photographers who are expected to have a world-wide audience of approximately four billion people.

- The Olympic Stadium was built within budget in a world record time of three years. It has 700 rooms and 112 panels of white material cover two-thirds of its spectator seats. The 80 000 seats are black and white. There is water on three sides of the stadium and it can be accessed by five bridges. Great care has been taken to make this building as sustainable as possible.

- When composing their three questions, encourage pupils to try to make them challenging so their peers need to read the text and deduce an answer rather than just locating a fact from the information provided. They can then work in small groups to ask other group members their questions. Each group can then select one interesting or challenging question for the whole class to answer.

- Research questions and answers can be collected and attached to a large sheet of paper or card and displayed.

answers

Teacher check

additional activities

- Pupils discuss why the Athletes' Village would be a good place to live after the Games and prepare a poster advertising the accommodation that will be available there for families.

- Research the sustainability of the Games in small groups to write a report. Add an evaluation, awarding a score out of 10 and giving reasons to support the awarding of this score.

Olympic Park

Although competitions will take place at many different locations both in and outside London during the Games, Olympic Park will be the major venue and focus for the Games. The spectacular Opening and Closing Ceremonies and the athletics will be staged at the Olympic Stadium in the Park. Spectators will watch aquatic sports, basketball, BMX riding, hockey, handball and track cycling at different venues within the park. It will also be home to the world's best athletes while they are in London and the International Broadcasting and Main Press Centres will also be located within this park.

However, it is not just a site for major new Games venues … it is so much more than that! The organisers decided to restore the wetlands of this old industrial site in eastern London to create Olympic Park. Water from the nearby River Lea was used to restore the habitat of native fauna and flora and to attract people, too. Thirty bridges will provide access to parklands and venues, and large outdoor screens will allow spectators to watch events as they happen.

The **Olympic Stadium** is a very exciting modern sports facility which can seat 80 000 people. The organisers planned to make it the most sustainable stadium ever built. They used concrete made from industrial waste to construct the lower section, which is seated in a bowl in the ground. Very light steel was used for the main construction and the top was made from leftover gas pipes.

The **Aquatics Centre**, with its wave-like roof, is located near the main entrance to Olympic Park (about 800 metres from Olympic Stadium). Many spectators will pass it on their way into the park. The Water Polo Centre is next to it and they share some facilities. Diving, swimming, synchronised swimming and the aquatics section of the modern pentathlon will all take place in one of three pools: one for swimming, one for diving and a 50-metre warm-up pool.

1. Write three questions about Olympic Park using the information on this page.

- _____

- _____

- _____

2. (a) Write one question about something you don't know about Olympic Park.

- _____

(b) Find the answer to your question.

- _____

weymouth and portland

objective

- Reads and understands information about the Olympic sailing venue, Weymouth and Portland.

teacher information

- Weymouth and Portland is a local government district (and borough) in Dorset, on the south coast of England. It is about 175.38 km south-west from London. Located inside Portland Harbour is the Weymouth and Portland National Sailing Academy, from where the Olympic sailing events will take place. This area was chosen as the Olympic sailing venue because of the good sailing conditions, and the fact that the Sailing Academy had only recently been built, so a new venue would not need to be constructed.

- Pupils will need to understand what a breakwater is before completing page 55. It is a protective stone or concrete barrier built on coasts at the entry into a body of water to protect the coast or harbour from large waves and strong currents.

bold words

- The bold words are more difficult words or terms that the pupils might need to discuss with the teacher or look up in a dictionary.

answers

(a) Weymouth and Portland was chosen for the sailing events because of the good sailing conditions, and the fact that the Sailing Academy, with it's new facilities, had only recently been built (so it was not necessary to build a new venue).

(b) In order to improve the pre-existing facilities, a new slipway and 70 marina berths were built.

(c) The pupils should shade the water sections of Portland Harbour and Weymouth Bay.

(d) The stone breakwaters protect the harbour from large waves and strong currents.

additional activities

- Pupils could research areas in Ireland that are renowned for sailing, such as Strangford Lough, Dublin Bay, or Wexford, Waterford and Cork Harbours.

- Discuss breakwaters. Why are they built, how do they work and in what ways do they impact upon the environment?

- Pupils find out more about the locality of Weymouth and Portland, and create a travel brochure or computer presentation to showcase the area.

Weymouth and Portland

1. Read the text.

Weymouth Bay is a **sheltered bay** in Dorset, on the south coast of England. Between Weymouth and nearby Portland Island is Portland Harbour, formed by **stone breakwaters** built between 1848 and 1905. It is one of the largest constructed harbours in the world.

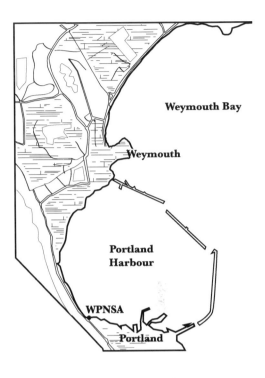

The harbour is ideal for sailing because it gets reliable winds from most directions, but is sheltered from large waves and strong **currents**. The Weymouth and Portland National Sailing Academy, located in the harbour, is a sailing centre that was built shortly before London was chosen to host the Games. This location, with its new facilities and excellent sailing conditions, was chosen to hold the sailing events for the Summer Olympics. Both the sheltered waters in Portland Harbour and the more challenging conditions in Weymouth Bay will be used for the sailing courses.

The facilities have been improved for the Olympics. A new **slipway** (a ramp on the shore to move ships or boats to and from the water) has been built, as have 70 marina **berths** (places in the harbour used to hold the boats while they are not at sea). The site has already hosted international sailing events and should prove to be an excellent venue for the sailing events at the Games.

2. Complete the following.

(a) Write two reasons Weymouth and Portland was chosen as the venue for the

Games' sailing events. _____

_____

_____

(b) What improvements have been made to the venue for the Olympics?

_____

_____

(c) With a blue pencil, shade the areas on the map where you think the sailing races will take place.

(d) How do the stone breakwaters contribute to the good sailing conditions at

Weymouth and Portland? _____

_____

old trafford

objective

- Reads and comprehends information about Old Trafford, one of the six venues for men's and women's football at the London 2012 Olympic Games.

teacher information

- Besides being home to the Manchester United Football Club (the Red Devils), Old Trafford has been the venue for important rugby league and rugby union matches, boxing events and used for games of shinty, the traditional game of the Scottish Highlands. It has also been used for several concerts, for performers such as Bruce Springsteen, Take That and Bon Jovi.

- Discuss what 'away fans' are. (Fans supporting the opposing team from another club—not fans for the home team.)

bold words

- Write each of the bold words in a meaningful sentence; e.g. parochial: 'The parochial Manchester United supporter wore a red shirt to work matching the team's jumper in the week leading up to the derby'.

answers

1. Teacher check
2. Boxes C, D and E
3. The West Stand should be coloured red. (Pupils should deduce from Box B that as Manchester United's nickname is the 'Red Devils' the team colour is red.)
4. Away fans and disabled fans (and their carers)
5. The rectangle should be drawn between the West and South Stand.
6. (a) False
   (b) True
   (c) False

additional activities

- Pupils can use an atlas or online map to locate Old Trafford.

- Take a virtual tour of Old Trafford at <http://www.manutd.com/en/Visit-Old-Trafford/Virtual-Tour.aspx>

- Find more about Old Trafford as a venue for Olympic football matches on the official London 2102 Olympic Games website: <http://www.london2012.com/old-trafford>

Old Trafford, one of the most famous football stadiums in the world, is one of six venues for the men's and women's football at the 2012 Games.

1. Read the information in the boxes and study the map of the venue, then complete the activities.

A Old Trafford is located in north-west England, a few kilometres from the city centre of Manchester.

B The stadium is home to Manchester United Football Club (Red Devils), the most **successful** football club in England.

C Old Trafford is an all-seater stadium with a capacity of **approximately** 76 000 spectators.

D Old Trafford 's current record **attendance** is 76 962 (set in 1939 when the stadium had standing room). The stadium has undergone several redevelopments since it first opened in February 1910. A second **tier**, planned for the South Stand, will raise the capacity to over 90 000.

OLD TRAFFORD STADIUM

North Stand

Tier 3
Tier 2
Upper
Lower

West Stand
East Stand

South Stand — Away fans

E After Wembley Stadium in north-west London, Old Trafford is the second largest football ground in England and the third largest in the United Kingdom.

F Old Trafford has the **nickname** of the 'Theatre of Dreams', given by Sir Bobby Charlton, a highly **regarded** Manchester United player of the 1950s to early 1970s.

G The best known stand is the West Stand or Stretford End Stand where traditionally the most **parochial** fans are located.

H Old Trafford has a section in the East Stand for 170 **disabled** fans, with free seats for carers.

I The players' tunnel is located in the south-west corner of the stadium.

2. Which box or boxes give information about the capacity and size of Old Trafford?

_____

3. On the map of the stadium, colour the stand that would hold the supporters who cheer loudest for Manchester United. Use Manchester United's team colour.

4. Who are two groups of fans that share the East Stand?

_____

5. On the map, draw a red rectangle over the area where the players' tunnel is located.

6. Answer TRUE or FALSE.

(a) Old Trafford will soon celebrate its 100th anniversary. .... ☐

(b) The stadium caters for fans in wheelchairs. .... ☐

(c) Old Trafford is fondly known as the 'Bobby Charlton Stadium'. .... ☐

OLYMPIC COUNCIL OF IRELAND

greenwich park

objective

- Reads, understands and summarises information about Greenwich Park, the Olympic venue for equestrian events and parts of the modern pentathlon events.

teacher information

- Greenwich (pronounced 'Gren-itch') Park is the venue for the Olympic equestrian events, parts of the modern pentathlon events, and the Paralympic dressage competition. Only the riding, shooting and running parts of the modern pentathlon will take place at Greenwich Park, with the swimming and fencing events taking place at venues in Olympic Park.

- Greenwich Park is about 7 kilometres from Olympic Park. This proximity is a key reason Greenwich was selected as the pentathlon venue; the pre-existing swimming and fencing venues can be combined with temporary venues at Greenwich Park, preventing the need to build a new, separate arena for the pentathlon.

bold words

- The bold words in the text are equestrian terms that the pupils could further investigate.

answers

What is Greenwich Park?	Greenwich Park is a large historic Royal Park in south-east London, on the south bank of the River Thames. It is home to several historic buildings, including the National Maritime Museum.
Where is Greenwich Park?	• Greenwich Park is in south-east London, on the south bank of the River Thames.
Which Olympic events will be held here?	• Equestrian events – dressage, jumping and eventing (including cross-country) • The riding, shooting and running elements of the modern pentathlon
Why was it chosen as an Olympic venue?	• It has enough space for the equestrian eventing discipline. • It is close to Olympic Park, making it easy for the athletes in the modern pentathlon to travel between events. • It has pre-existing venues, and allows equestrian and modern pentathlon events to be held in the same location, avoiding the need to build new or duplicate facilities, thereby reducing costs and saving resources.
How will it be turned into an Olympic venue?	Two of the following: • A temporary arena has been built within the grounds of the National Maritime Museum, including seating for approximately 23 000 people. • A temporary cross-country course will be built through the park. • Temporary stables will be built to house the horses.

additional activities

- Pupils could find out about Greenwich Mean Time, (a term originally referring to mean solar time at the Royal Observatory in Greenwich). In the United Kingdom, Greenwich Mean Time (zero-plus hours) is the official time during winter.

- Discuss why local Greenwich residents might object to the park being used as the venue for equestrian events (suggestions may include park closures, road closures, pollution and possible negative effects on the park's flora and fauna).

2012 Irish Olympic Team in London

58

www.prim-ed.com   Prim-Ed Publishing

Greenwich Park

Greenwich Park is a historic Royal Park in south-east London, on the south bank of the River Thames. It covers about 74 hectares and is home to several historic buildings, including the National Maritime Museum. The park is the venue for the equestrian and three sports of the modern pentathlon events for the Games.

Olympic equestrian events require an arena for **dressage** and **jumping**, and space for a **cross-country** course. A temporary arena has been built within the grounds of the National Maritime Museum, including seating for approximately 23 000 people. A temporary cross-country course has been designed to go through the park, and temporary stables will be built to house the horses.

The modern pentathlon has five elements (shooting, fencing, swimming, show jumping and running), all completed on one day. Athletes need the venues for these different parts to be close together. Greenwich Park is close to Olympic Park (where the fencing and swimming facilities are), making it easier for the athletes to travel from place to place. The riding, shooting and running elements of the modern pentathlon will be held at Greenwich Park.

By using the pre-existing venues, and holding the equestrian and modern pentathlon events in the same location in Greenwich Park, this avoids the need to build new or duplicate facilities, thereby reducing costs and saving resources. The central location of Greenwich Park will also allow spectators easy access to the venue by public transport.

Sort the information in the text above into the chart below. You need at least one piece of information per bullet point.

What is Greenwich Park?	•
Where is Greenwich Park?	•
Which Olympic events will be held here?	• •
Why was it chosen as an Olympic venue?	• • •
How will it be turned into an Olympic venue?	• •

Lord's Cricket Ground

Objective

- Reads and demonstrates understanding of text about Lord's Cricket Ground by composing questions and providing appropriate paragraph subtitles.

Teacher information

- There will be 128 archers (64 men and 64 women) competing for four medals at Lord's Cricket Ground, the 'home of cricket'.

- The current Lord's Cricket Ground is the third site chosen by the Marylebone Cricket Club (MCC) in their quest to find a place that was quiet and afforded them some privacy in the vicinity of St John's Wood in 1814. It was originally the site of a duck pond. Once the ground was established, the grass was kept trimmed by a flock of sheep. The first lawnmower was purchased for the club in 1864.

- Lord's Cricket Ground and the MCC have played a very important role in the development of cricket and how it *should be* played around the world. They controlled many aspects of the game, including the rules, until the creation of the International Cricket Council.

- Not a lot of work is necessary to prepare this beautiful cricket ground for the archery events at the Games. The temporary stands that will be erected along both sides of the archery range should afford most of the 6500 spectators an excellent view of the archers and their targets.

- Although there is quite a slope across the cricket ground (more than 2.4 metres), the archery range has been positioned in such a way as to minimise its effect.

- The J.P. Morgan Media Centre, opposite the Pavilion, is a state-of-the-art facility. Its striking modern architecture has won awards and it has been acclaimed one of the best buildings in Great Britain. It is a most unusual building and a surprising contrast to the traditional architecture of Lord's pavilion.

- It is likely that many of the spectators—especially those from Australia, New Zealand, India, Pakistan, the West Indies, Sri Lanka and other cricketing nations—will welcome the opportunity to visit this famous cricket ground.

- The archery equipment being used at Lord's during these events will be donated to archery clubs and schools at the conclusion of the Games.

- Visit:

    – <http://www.theashescricketlive.com/ashes-history/> for an explanation of 'the Ashes.'

    – <http://www.lords.org/history/mcc-history/> for information about the history of Lord's.

    – <http://www.youtube.com/watch?v=ZEWw5hCMzTw> for a virtual tour of the Media Centre.

    – <http://www.youtube.com/watch?v=DfDV1zjpXqQ> for interviews about archery at Lord's.

Answers

1. Teacher check
2. Teacher check

Additional activities

- There is a court at Lord's where 'real tennis' is played. It is part of the tour. Research 'real tennis' and record similarities and differences between this ancient 'game of kings' and lawn tennis.

- Write six interesting facts about Lord's and explain why you would or wouldn't want to go there.

- Discuss possible reasons why the Olympic organisers have limited the number of spectators permitted to watch archery at Lord's.

Lord's Cricket Ground

Introduction

Lord's Cricket Ground, one of the most famous sporting venues in the world, will be the setting for the men's and women's Olympic archery competitions. It is located at St John's Wood, only a short walk from the London Underground station near Regent's Park.

Lord's, as it is usually known, has been the 'home of cricket' since 1814. It was named after Thomas Lord, a bowler who purchased the land and set it up as a cricket ground for the Marylebone Cricket Club (MCC), which is still based at Lord's and now owns it. This famous club set down the rules of cricket in what is known as the 'Code of Laws' and organised the first 'Ashes' tour to Australia.

Lord's is a popular tourist attraction and visitors can view the Pavilion, built in 1890. Tours include the famous dressing rooms with historic honour boards and the Long Room, which players walk though on their way to the pitch and back. This room provides members of the MCC with an excellent view and features an art gallery with portraits of famous cricketers. The MCC Museum, believed to be the world's oldest sports museum, is in the Pavilion. The Ashes, the highly-prized trophy English cricketers have battled with Australia over since 1882, is on display there. Other attractions include the futuristic J.P. Morgan Media Centre, the indoor cricket school, and tennis courts (where the game of 'real tennis', played by King Henry VIII, is still played).

Lord's can accommodate 28 000 spectators, but numbers will be capped at only 6500 for the four archery events of the Games. Archers will shoot from in front of the Pavilion, towards the Media Centre. Two temporary stands for spectators will be set up in that half of the ground, parallel with the range.

1. Write a suitable subtitle at the top of the box for each paragraph of the text.

2. Write a question that is answered in each paragraph.

Paragraph 1.	Subtitle: _____ Introduction _____
Paragraph 2.	Subtitle: _____
Paragraph 3.	Subtitle: _____
Paragraph 4.	Subtitle: _____

the mall

objectives

- Reads information about The Mall in London.
- Writes questions for given answers using the text provided.

teacher information

- The Mall (pronounced 'Mal') is the (approximately) 1 km-long road between Buckingham Palace and Trafalgar Square. The Mall starts at the Victoria Memorial (on a roundabout in front of Buckingham Palace) and goes through Admiralty Arch.

- The Mall was created as a ceremonial route. It is closed to traffic on Sundays and public holidays, and during ceremonial occasions.

- During the London Games, the marathon, race walk and cycling road races will start and finish in The Mall. The Paralympic marathon will also start and finish at The Mall. For these events, temporary seating, video screens, tents and scoreboards will be erected.

bold words

- Croquet is a game played by knocking wooden balls through a series of iron arches with a mallet.

- Iron oxides are chemical compounds composed of iron and oxygen. Rust is a reddish-brown compound of iron and oxygen.

- A pigment is a dry substance, usually pulverised, which becomes a paint, ink or dye when mixed with water (or other liquid).

answers

The exact wording of the questions that are written will differ slightly from pupil to pupil, but should contain the same basic information as those listed below.

1. What colour is the surface of The Mall?
2. What is the name of the game (played along a track in St James's Park that the Mall roughly follows) that The Mall got its name from?
3. Which three Olympic events will start and finish in The Mall?
4. What is the red colouring of the surface of The Mall intended to give the impression of?
5. What pigment gives The Mall its red colour?
6. Which two of London's famous landmarks does The Mall connect?

additional activities

- Pupils could find out more about iron oxide. What is it? What is it used for?

- Discuss red carpets, and when and why they are used. Make a list of events that use red carpets.

- Compare The Mall (length, width, age, number of famous landmarks) with other famous ceremonial roads or avenues, such as the National Mall in Washington D.C., the Champs-Elysées in Paris, the Rajpath in New Delhi, O'Connell Street in Dublin, or Unter den Linden in Berlin.

The Mall

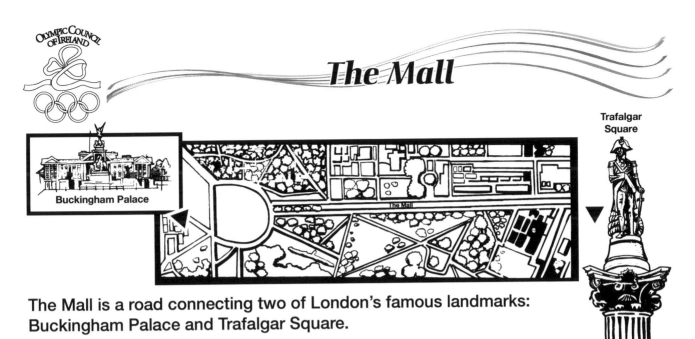

Trafalgar Square

Buckingham Palace

The Mall is a road connecting two of London's famous landmarks: Buckingham Palace and Trafalgar Square.

The Mall was built between the late 19th and early 20th centuries. The name of the road comes from a game called *paille-maille* or pall mall (similar to **croquet**), which was played along a track in St James's Park that The Mall now roughly follows. The Mall was created as a ceremonial route for important ceremonies and grand parades.

The surface of The Mall is intentionally coloured red from an **iron oxide pigment**, to give the impression of a giant red carpet leading up to Buckingham Palace.

Today, The Mall acts as a normal road from Monday to Saturday. It is closed to traffic on Sundays and ceremonial occasions when it is decked out with flags. Important visiting foreign guests and members of the British royal family (for special occasions) are driven along The Mall to the Palace. The Mall is also the location for the finish of the annual London Marathon. During the 2012 Olympics, the marathon, race walking and cycling road races will start and finish in The Mall.

Write a question for each answer using the information in the text.

Question	Answer
1.	red
2.	paille-maille (or pall mall)
3.	marathon, race walking and cycling road races
4.	a giant red carpet
5.	iron oxide
6.	Buckingham Palace and Trafalgar Square

wembley stadium

objective

- Reads and demonstrates understanding of text by completing a crossword.

teacher information

- The venue for both the women's and men's gold medal football is Wembley Stadium. It is located 10 kilometres north-west of central London and is accessible by bus, and underground and overground rail. This impressive new stadium has been described as 'the first of its kind' and its designers believe that there is nothing else like it. After many delays, it was opened just in time for the FA (Football Association) Cup Final in 2007. It can seat 90 000 people and was built on the site of the former Wembley Stadium, (also known as Empire Stadium).

- Built by an Australian company, Multiplex, at a cost of 798 million pounds, (which was double its original budget), this modern stadium has many outstanding features. These include the comfort and positioning of the striking red seating, its partially retractable roof and the Wembley Arch, which soars so far above the stadium that it requires beacon lighting for low-flying aircraft. This arch is the longest single-span steel roof structure in the world. It is 134 metres high and spans 317 metres; its diameter is greater than that of a Channel Tunnel train. The world-class facilities of the stadium include many beautiful restaurants and 2618 toilets; (a world record for a building).

- Although Wembley Stadium was built for football, it is ideally suited to other huge events. There have been some memorable concerts there including the Live Earth Concert, and the Concert for Diana, (commemorating Diana, the Princess of Wales' life 10 years after she was fatally injured in Paris). *Madonna*, *Coldplay*, *Take That* and *U2* are some of the world-renown entertainers who have performed in front of huge crowds at Wembley Stadium.

- Wembley Stadium was designed by Lord Norman Foster and a virtual tour with him can be viewed at <http://www.youtube.com/watch?v=YIypEdIqmlI>.

answers

1. See crossword solution.

additional activities

- Use the internet to research information and statistics about an important football match that has been played at Wembley Stadium. Present a written or an oral report about this event to the class.

- Discuss and compile a list of possible reasons why Wembley Stadium was chosen as the venue for the women's and men's gold medal games.

- Imagine your national football association is offering two tickets to London to attend one of the gold medal events at Wembley Stadium. Write a letter to them explaining why you would like to see Wembley Stadium, which event you would most like to see and why you should win this valuable prize.

Wembley Stadium

Read about Wembley Stadium and find words in the boxes to help you to complete the crossword below.

The women's and the men's gold medal football matches will be played at Wembley Stadium.

Wembley Stadium is 10 kilometres north-west of central London. You can travel there by bus, the Tube or train.

The stadium has a partially retractable roof. The Wembley Arch soars 134 metres above it. It is so high, it has lights to warn low-flying aircraft on it. The diameter of the arch is greater than the Channel Tunnel train.

When England won the Football World Cup in 1966, Sir Bobby Moore was the captain. There is a big statue of him at the entrance of the new stadium.

Concerts are also held at Wembley. Stars like Madonna, Coldplay and U2 have performed there and it was the venue for the Concert for Diana.

There is comfortable seating for 90 000 people, who all have an excellent view of the pitch.

The Royal Box is where members of the British royal family sit. Winners have to walk up 107 steps to receive their medals and trophies.

The stadium was built on the site of the former Wembley Stadium. It was opened in 2007 and cost 798 million pounds.

Across

4. Prizes won in competition
5. Place where events are held
8. Large sports arena
11. Not losers
13. The line through the centre of a circle
14. Able to be pulled back

Down

1. Image of a person
2. Curved structure
3. There are 107 of them
6. Opposite of south
7. Machine that flies
9. Way in
10. Public musical performance
12. Earlier or past

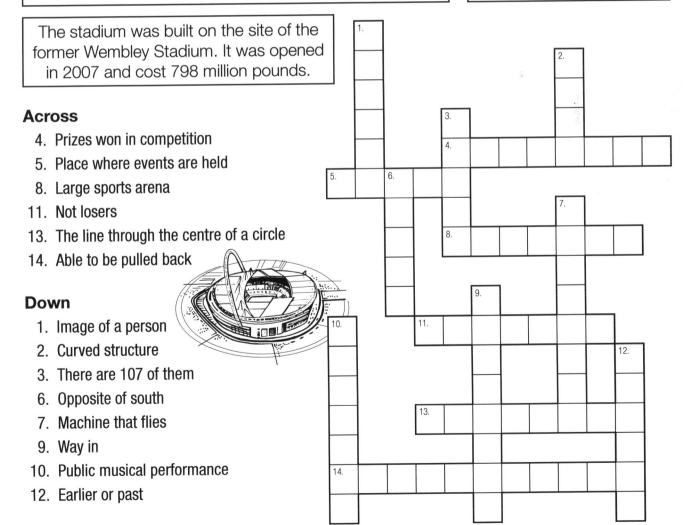

aquatics

objective

- Reads and comprehends information about the sport of aquatics at the 2012 Games.

teacher information

- Four disciplines make up the sport of aquatics: swimming, diving, synchronised swimming and water polo.

- Men and women both compete in 17 swimming events involving four strokes; the only difference is a men-only 1500 m freestyle event and a women-only 800 m freestyle event. (Refer to *<http://www.olympic.org/swimming-equipment-and-history>* for a list of all events.) Individual and team medley events involve swimming all four strokes in the one race. (Note: Freestyle is an unregulated swimming style used in swimming competitions, but the front crawl is usually swum as it is the fastest. As such, the term 'freestyle' is often used as a synonym for the front crawl.)

answers

Page 67

(Note: Answers refer to swimming at Olympic standard)

1. (a) *freestyle:* on starting blocks in dive position; prone (facedown), alternate overarm movements; alternate up and down flutter kick movements; tumble turn (somersault in front of wall and push off with feet); hit touch pad with one hand

   (b) *breaststroke:* on starting blocks in dive position; prone, hands and arms move forward at same time then outward and rearward from in front of chest; in a frog-like motion (more of a 'whip kick' motion at top level); both hands touch the wall before swimmer turns and kicks off wall with feet; hit touch pad with both hands simultaneously

   (c) *backstroke:* in water hanging on to starting grips with knees bent and feet on wall, upright (faceup); alternate backward movement of arms, alternate up and down flutter kick movements, tumble turn; hit touch pad with one hand

   (d) *butterfly:* on starting blocks in dive position; prone, arms lifted together out of water then brought backward simultaneously; up and down movements in dolphin kick; both hands touch the wall before swimmer turns and kicks off wall with feet; hit touch pad with both hands simultaneously

Page 68

Diving: 1. individual, platform 2. synchronised, same 3. dive 4. twists 5. ten, water 6. splash

Synchronised swimming: 1. Women 2. performing 3. ballet 4. awarded 5. pool 6. prevent 7. eggbeater

e	m	p	r	e	v	e	n	t	b	p	t	e	n
t	i	n	d	i	v	i	d	u	a	l	g	u	u
t	w	m	m	b	r	v	i	s	l	a	s	n	w
w	a	t	e	r	n	k	v	q	l	t	a	c	o
i	x	a	w	a	r	d	e	d	e	f	c	p	m
s	f	j	o	i	m	b	e	e	t	o	y	o	e
t	y	e	g	g	b	e	a	t	e	r	g	o	n
s	p	l	a	s	h	i	n	s	a	m	e	l	s
p	e	r	f	o	r	m	i	n	g	i	n	g	e
d	s	y	n	c	h	r	o	n	i	s	e	d	l

Page 69

1. (a) 7   (b) 6   (c) 1   (d) 3
2. True
3. False
4. 30
5. red
6. 20
7. A wet pass lands in the water and a dry pass is caught before it hits the water.
8. Yes
9. A race for the ball in the centre of the area of play to start each quarter.
10. 8 minutes

additional activities

- Find out how the individual medley swimming events and medley relays are structured.

- Follow the individual and synchronised diving competitions and the synchronised swimming competitions and work out how the scores are given and the eventual winners are determined. Compare to artistic and rhythmic gymnastic scoring.

Aquatics – Swimming

Swimming is one of the four disciplines in the sport of aquatics at the 2012 Games. There are four different strokes, which are used in a variety of races.

1. Research to summarise the main similarities and differences among the four strokes. Use keywords and phrases. The following websites will help you:

- *<http://www.london2012.com/swimming>*

- *<http://www.olympic.org/swimming-equipment-and-history>*

- *<http://assets.olympic.org/SportAnimations/en/summer/SW/SW_EN.html>*

	(a)	(b)	(c)	(d)
Name of stroke				
Where and in what position do swimmers begin the race?				
Position of body during race				
Description of arm motion				
Description of leg motion				
How must swimmers turn at the end of a lap?				
How must swimmers end the race?				

Aquatics – Diving and synchronised swimming

Learn some interesting facts about the aquatic disciplines of diving and synchronised swimming by completing the sentences. Answers can be found in the wordsearch. The first letter of each missing word is provided as a clue.

e	m	p	r	e	v	e	n	t	b	p	t	e	n
t	i	n	d	i	v	i	d	u	a	l	g	u	u
t	w	m	m	b	r	v	i	s	l	a	s	n	w
w	a	t	e	r	n	k	v	q	l	t	a	c	o
i	x	a	w	a	r	d	e	d	e	f	c	p	m
s	f	j	o	i	m	b	e	e	t	o	y	o	e
t	y	e	g	g	b	e	a	t	e	r	g	o	n
s	p	l	a	s	h	i	n	s	a	m	e	l	s
p	e	r	f	o	r	m	i	n	g	i	n	g	e
d	s	y	n	c	h	r	o	n	i	s	e	d	l

Synchronised swimming

1. W_____ only compete, in duet (two) and team (eight) events.

2. Synchronised swimming involves

   p_____ routines in a pool to music and in perfect harmony.

3. It is described as being b_____ in water.

4. Marks are a_____ out of a possible 10 for artistic impression and for technical merit.

5. Swimmers are not allowed to touch the

   bottom of the p_____.

6. Nose clips are worn to

   p_____ water from entering the nose.

7. Movements include the

   e_____, barracuda, rocket twist and flamingo.

Diving

1. Male and female divers compete in

   i_____ and synchronised events on the 3 m springboard and

   10 m p_____.

2. In s_____ diving, two divers complete the same dive at the

   s_____ time.

3. Each d_____ is scored depending partly on the difficulty of the manoeuvres attempted.

4. Manoeuvres include somersaults, pikes,

   t_____ and tucks.

5. Judges watch each dive and give a

   score out of t_____. They look at each diver's approach, take-off, style and entry into the

   w_____. Points are adjusted for the degree of difficulty.

6. Divers try to make as little a

   s_____ as possible upon entry.

Aquatics – Water polo

Water polo is one of the four disciplines in the sport of aquatics at the London Games. Research to find the answers to this water polo quiz and see how many points you score out of 15. The following websites will help you:

- *<http://www.london2012.com/waterpolo>*
- *<http://assets.olympic.org/SportAnimations/en/summer/WP/WP_EN.html>*
- *<http://www.olympic.org/water-polo-equipment-and-history>*

1. How many:

   (a) players in each team? _____ (1 pt)

   (b) substitutes for each team? _____ (1 pt)

   (c) goalkeepers in each team? _____ (1 pt)

   (d) attackers in a team? _____ (1 pt)

2. Men's and women's teams compete at Olympic Games.

| TRUE / FALSE |
(1 pt)

3. All players can touch the bottom and sides of the pool.

| TRUE / FALSE |
(1 pt)

4. A team has _____ seconds to attempt to score a goal before a free throw is given to the opposition. (1 pt)

5. What colour cap does a goalkeeper wear?

| RED / BLUE / WHITE |
(1 pt)

6. For how many seconds can a player be excluded for committing a serious foul?

_____ seconds (1 pt)

7. What is the difference between a wet and a dry pass? (2 pt)

_____

_____

_____

8. Is the goalkeeper allowed to use both hands when playing the ball?

| YES / NO |
(1 pt)

9. What is meant by the term 'swim-off'? (2 pt)

_____

_____

_____

10. How long does each quarter last?

_____ (1 pt)

How did you do?

Question	1	2	3	4	5	6	7	8	9	10	Total
Score											/15

archery

objective

- Reads and comprehends information about the sport of archery at the 2012 Games.

teacher information

- Lord's Cricket Ground, the 'home of cricket' since 1814, will host the archery competition at the Games. An archery range will be constructed on the outfield of the main ground. Approximately 6500 spectators will be able to view the action in temporary stands.

- Recurve bows are the only bows used in Olympic archery. They are named for their side-view profile. A recurve (or classic) bow has tips that curve up and away from the archer when the bow is unstrung. The string touches sections of the limbs when the bow is strung. This type of bow stores more energy than a straight-limbed bow. The recurve shape makes the bow shorter than a simple bow and, therefore, less difficult for archers on horseback to use.

- The arrow length is chosen according to the archer's reach. Arrows are made from aluminium or carbon graphite. Aluminium arrows are more uniform in weight and shape, and graphite arrows fly faster.

- Various protective equipment is worn by the archers. This includes a chestguard made of leather or plastic to protect against a body injury when a bowstring is released, and a finger tab to protect the fingers when an arrow is drawn or released.

- To be a first-class archer, an athlete needs to have good upper body strength to control the bow and arrow, excellent technique, steady hands, sharp eyes for aiming at the target, and the ability to concentrate extremely well for long periods.

- Note: pupils will need to access the glossary at <http://www.olympic.org/archery-equipment-and-history> to find 'spotter'—the last clue in the crosspatch.

bold words

- Use a class or online dictionary to write a definition for each word.

   Stone Age: *the time when early humans lived in which they made tools from stone and flint*

   weapons: *instruments for fighting; e.g. spears, firearms*

   recreational: *relating to a game, hobby or sport participated in for enjoyment purposes*

   concentric: *having the same centre*

   specific: *particular*

   challenging: *engaging in a contest*

answers

1. (a) | b | o | w | s | t | r | i | n | g |

   (b) | t | a | r | g | e | t |

   (c) | n | o | c | k |

   (d) | a | r | m | g | u | a | r | d |

   (e) | a | r | r | o | w |

   (f) | q | u | i | v | e | r |

   (g) | s | p | o | t | t | e | r |

2. recurve

additional activity

- In pairs, pupils use a compass to construct an archery target on paper. They write the numbers 1 to 10 in the correct circles. On a separate sheet of paper, they write six numbers underneath each other between 0 and 30. These numbers represent the total score an individual archer could have made in shooting sets of three arrows. Pupils then work out one way the 'archer' could have achieved each score with his or her three arrows; e.g. 30: 10, 10, 10; 25: 7, 8, 10.

Archery

Archery is a sport that uses a bow and arrow to hit a target. The use of bows and arrows dates back more than 10 000 years to the **Stone Age**, when they were first used in hunting and, later, in warfare. When firearms replaced bows and arrows as **weapons**, archery gradually became a **recreational** sport.

In Olympic archery, archers use a bow and arrow to shoot at a target 70 metres away. The 'draw weight' of the bow (the amount of weight the archer pulls when he or she draws back on the bow) is about 20 kilograms. The target is 1.22 metres in diameter and has 10 **concentric** rings and a circle. Points are scored depending in which ring the archer's arrow lands in. An arrow in the outermost ring will score 1 point, while an arrow in the innermost circle or ring (bullseye) will score 10 points. An arrow landing on the dividing line between rings is given the higher of the two scores.

The rings are coloured in a **specific** way. In order from the outermost ring, these are: two white, two black, two blue, two red, two gold and a gold centre circle. The gold rings in the centre are 12.2 centimetres in diameter.

There are team and individual events for men and women at the Olympic Games. Individual archery matches will be competed over the best of five sets, with each set consisting of three arrows for each archer. Team competitions consist of three archers per team, with each team **challenging** each other in the 'best of 24 arrows' format.

1. Use the following websites to help you find the answers to the clues in the crosspatch about archery equipment and find the vertical hidden word.

   - <http://www.olympic.org/archery-equipment-and-history>
   - <http://assets.olympic.org/SportAnimations/en/summer/AR/AR_EN.html>
   - <http://www.london2012.com/archery>

   (a) String of a bow.
   (b) This is 70 m away from archer.
   (c) Notch at end of arrow.
   (d) Protects the arm from being hit by the bowstring after an arrow is shot.
   (e) Can travel at more than 240 km/h.
   (f) Container for holding arrows.
   (g) Person who identifies each archer's score with a telescopic sight.

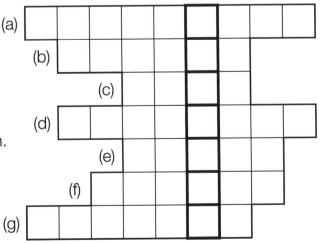

2. The hidden word is: _____.
   (This is the only type of bow used in Olympic competition.)

athletics

objectives

- Answers questions to show understanding of the four disciplines of athletics.

- Researches to find differences in equipment used by men and women in some athletics events.

teacher information

- Athletics events are the oldest form of organised sport. They began with the simplest physical activities of running, throwing and jumping and evolved into the events we know today.

- The unusual dimensions of equipment is a result of the change from imperial to metric measure. If the dimensions were altered, new sets of records would have to be instated.

- Women have not always been able to compete in so many athletics events. The triple jump was introduced at the Atlanta Games in 1996, the hammer throw and pole vault at Sydney in 2000, and the steeplechase at Beijing in 2008.

answers

Page 74

1. track, field, combined and road

2. The hurdles are taller in the men's event, which is over 110 m. The women's event is over 100 m.

3. (a) 28   (b) 7

4. (a) running races, long jump, triple jump, high jump, pole vault, marathon, 20 km walk

   (b) The conditions for these events are the same for men and women.

5. The 110 m hurdle event finishing times would be faster because this is a specialised event for these athletes. Decathletes spread their effort over more events so they would not be expected to achieve such good times as those who only practise hurdling.

6. An athlete who scores well in all events, against an athlete who scores well in some events but poorly in others, will achieve a higher total score.

7. discus and pole vault

8. (a) 110 m hurdles, decathlon, 50 km walk

   (b) 100 m hurdles, heptathlon

9. Keep contact with the ground at all times

Page 75

1. (a) Sprint hurdles: men – 1.067 m, women – 0.84 m; 400 m hurdles: men – 0.914 m, women – 0.762 m; Steeplechase: men – 0.914 m, women – 0.762 m

   (b) Steeplechase hurdles are solid so they do not fall down when athletes step on them as they jump over.

   (c) Discus: weight – men 2 kg, women 1 kg; diameter – men 22 cm, women 18 cm

   Javelin: weight – men minimum 800 g, women minimum 600 g; length – men between 2.6 and 2.7 m, women between 2.2 and 2.3 m

   (d) Shot: weight – men 7.3 kg, women 4 kg; Hammer: weight – men 7.3 kg, women 4 kg

   (e) A hammer has three main parts; the ball or 'head' which is attached to a length of steel wire (maximum 1.215 m) with a grip or 'handle' at the end. This is the only throwing event in which the competitor may wear gloves. The hammer is swung above the head for three or four turns to gain maximum speed before release. The speed of the ball and the angle from the ground at its release point determine the distance the ball will travel.

additional activities

- Write a detailed report on an athletics event. Include sketches of equipment and other diagrams to clarify information. Explain scoring and rules for starting, heats, rounds and disqualification.

- For each athletics event, find the gold, silver and bronze medallists from the Olympics in 2004 and 2008. Draw up a table with their names and flags of the nations they represent. Leave a space in the table to record the medal winners from the London Games.

Athletics

Although athletics is billed as one sport, represented by a single pictograph, it consists of four disciplines. Olympic Stadium is the venue for the track, field and combined disciplines. The road events take place on the streets of central London, finishing at The Mall.

Track events

Running races, from the 100 m sprint to the 10 000 m long distance event, are contested under equal conditions by men and women, but the 10 hurdles in each of the 100 m (women), 110 m (men) and 400 m (men and women) events are taller for men than for women.

In the $7\frac{1}{2}$-lap steeplechase events, the first 200 m are run with no obstacles. The five hurdles on each lap are the same height as those used in the 400 m events. One of the hurdles includes a water jump.

Field events

The four jumps (long, triple, high and pole vault) are also contested under equal conditions by men and women. There are no rules governing the weight and length of a pole, but the missiles of the four throwing events (shot-put, discus, javelin and hammer) vary in weight and diameter or length for each gender.

Combined events

The decathlon for men and the heptathlon for women combine a selection of track and field competitions into one event. Each event is held over two consecutive days. The points scored by an athlete in each part are then totalled. The athlete with the greatest number of points after the ten or seven parts wins the Olympic title.

Because points are awarded for times and distance rather than placement in the field, it is possible for an athlete to win the overall event without having won any of the components. Faster times and greater distances receive more points.

Decathlon		Heptathlon	
Day one	**Day two**	**Day one**	**Day two**
1. 100 m sprint	6. 110 m hurdles	1. 100 m hurdles	5. long jump
2. long jump	7. discus	2. high jump	6. javelin
3. shot-put	8. pole vault	3. shot-put	7. 800 m race
4. high jump	9. javelin	4. 200 m sprint	
5. 400 m sprint	10. 1500 m race		

Road events

In addition to the marathon and the 20 km walk (in which both men and women compete), there is a men-only 50 km walk.

It is possible for a marathon runner to stop and walk (or even hop, jump and skip if he or she so chooses), but a race walker must have contact with the ground at all times. Enforcing this rule is very difficult and has led to many controversial disqualifications.

Use the text on page 73 to answer the questions.

1. The four disciplines of athletics are:

2. How do the sprint hurdle events differ for men as compared to women?

_____

_____

3. In the 3000 m steeplechase, an athlete jumps

    (a) a standard hurdle _____ times; and

    (b) a water jump _____ times.

4. (a) In which athletics events could men and women compete against each other

      equally? _____

    _____

    (b) Explain why. _____

    _____

5. How do you think the finishing times would compare between the men's 110 m hurdles event and 110 m hurdles component of the decathlon? Explain your answer.

_____

_____

6. How is it possible for a decathlete or pentathlete to win the gold medal without winning any of the component events?

_____

_____

7. Which field events are part of the decathlon but not the heptathlon?

_____

8. (a) What are three athletics events that women do not compete in?

    _____

    (b) What are the two athletics events that men do not compete in?

    _____

9. What must a walker do to avoid disqualification?

_____

Athletics

Most types of athletic events are contested by both men and women, but the dimensions of equipment used in hurdle and throwing events by each gender do vary.

1. Research to find the information.

(a) Find the height of hurdles used by men and women in each event.

Sprint hurdles		400 m hurdles		Steeplechase	
Men 110 m	Women 100 m	Men	Women	Men	Women

(b) What is the major difference between the hurdles used for the 400 m hurdle event and for the 3000 m steeplechase event?

_____

_____

(c) Find the weight and diameter of the discus, and weight and length of the javelin used by men and women in each event.

Discus				Javelin			
Weight		Diameter		Weight		Length	
Men	Women	Men	Women	Men	Women	Men	Women

(d) Find the weight of the shot-put and hammer used by men and women in each event.

(e) Draw a labelled diagram of the hammer and describe how it is thrown.

Shot-put		Hammer	
Weight		Weight	
Men	Women	Men	Women

OLYMPIC COUNCIL OF IRELAND

Basketball

Objective

- Reads information about basketball and uses information to complete activities.

Teacher Information

- Physical education professor Dr James Naismith was looking for a way to keep his gym class active and fit on a rainy day in December 1891. He wrote some basic rules, nailed a peach basket 10-feet (3.05 m) from the ground, got a football and the game of basketball began.

- The baskets were originally nailed to a balcony, but when spectators on the balcony began to interfere with shots the backboard was introduced.

- There are five standard basketball positions:

  point guard – the main ball handler and normally the best passer on the team

  shooting guard – similar to the point guard, but usually the team's best scorer

  small forward – not actually small (taller than the shooting guard but not as tall as the power forward), a well-balanced player with good shooting, defending, passing and rebounding skills

  power forward – usually strongest defender, guards the basket

  centre – usually the tallest player, blocks shots at goal, gets rebounds and scores.

Bold Words

- The bold words are the five basketball positions and the skills used in basketball. Pupils will need to use these words to complete the activity at the bottom of the page.

Answers

1.–2. Players from left to right:

First player is the shooting guard; this player is shooting.

Second player is the point guard; this player is passing.

Third player is the small forward; this player is dribbling the ball.

Fourth player is the centre; this player is shooting.

Fifth player is the power forward; this player is defending.

Additional Activities

- Basketball may have been loosely based on a game called 'duck on a rock'. Play this game with the pupils, then ask them to compare and contrast the two games. 'Duck on a rock' is played with one player standing guard over a 'stone on a rock' (teachers would need to use other objects instead of stones, such as a basketball balanced on a cone), while the other players attempt to knock it off by throwing small 'stones' (tennis balls) at it. Once it is knocked off, the throwers run in to retrieve their 'stones'. If a player is tagged before returning to the throwing line with his or her 'stones', they become the guard. The guard has to pick up the 'duck' (basketball) and put it back onto the rock (cone) before he or she can tag anyone. If a thrower is tagged by the guard while trying to recover his or her 'stone', he or she becomes the guard.

- Pupils can find out the history of a favourite sport: finding out where and when the game started, and how it has changed since its beginnings.

Basketball

Where do baskets, shots and dribbles come together? In the game of basketball! Invented in 1891, the game which originally involved throwing footballs into wooden peach baskets is now one of the most popular in the world. It was first played as an Olympic event at the Berlin 1936 Olympic Games, with women's basketball introduced at the 1976 Games in Montreal.

In the game, two teams of five players try to score points by throwing a ball into the opponent's basket, while trying to prevent the other team from scoring. There are five positions:

> **the point guard:** usually the team's best ball handler and passer and often the smallest player in the team
>
> **the shooting guard:** usually the team's best shooter, able to shoot goals from long range
>
> **the small forward:** often slightly shorter, quicker and leaner than other forward and centre players, they are quick and have good ball skills
>
> **the power forward:** similar to the centre, only taller. They often play under the basket in defence
>
> **the centre:** usually the tallest player, playing close to the basket.

Players need to **pass** (throw or bounce the ball to another player), **shoot** (throw the basketball toward the hoop) or **dribble** (bounce the ball on the floor continuously with one hand while walking or running down the court) the ball. They also need to **defend** (try to get the ball from the other team and stop them scoring).

1. On the line with an arrow, label that player's position.
2. In the boxes, write the name of the skill (pass, shoot, dribble or defend) being shown.

Boxing

objective

• Reads information about boxing and uses the information to complete activities.

teacher information

• Boxing is a sport in which two athletes of approximately the same weight fight each other with their fists in an area called a ring. It is supervised by a referee and typically consists of a series of short rounds. The ring is square, with posts in each corner connected by three or four tightly drawn ropes.

• Boxers at the Olympics must wear gloves, a protective head guard, and a mouthpiece to protect their body. Scores are given by five judges, with one point given for each valid punch made to an opponent's head or upper body. A referee ensures that the boxers follow the rules, and can stop the fight at any time if he or she thinks a boxer is not able to continue. At the end of each round, each boxer goes back to his or her corner to rest for one minute. The winner is the boxer with the most points. If a boxer is knocked down, the other boxer must immediately cease fighting and move to the furthest neutral corner of the ring until the referee has either ruled a knockout or called for the fight to continue.

• Professional (as opposed to amateur boxing, practised at the Olympic and Commonwealth Games) has its own set of rules and a different scoring system. In the Olympics, men have three three-minute rounds, while women have four two-minute rounds. Boxers score points for every punch they land successfully on their opponent's head or upper body.

• The Olympic boxing competition will feature 10 men's weight categories, while the women's competition will have three weights: flyweight, lightweight and middleweight.

bold word

• Pupils can find out why the boxing ring, although square, is called a ring. Try <*http://whitecollarboxing. com/boxinfo.htm*>. (Contests were originally fought in a roughly drawn circle on the ground.)

answers

1. The post and boxer in the left-hand corner should be coloured red. The post and boxer diagonally opposite the red boxer should be coloured blue.

2. Boxing gloves are padded to protect the hands of the boxer and to reduce the damage done to an opponent.

3. A flyweight who gained 4 kg would have to fight in the bantamweight division.

4. A boxer scores a point during an Olympic bout when he or she hits the opponent with the white section of their gloves on the front or sides of the opponent's body (above the belt) or head.

additional activities

• Working in small groups, pupils could have a verbal boxing match (a debate). Once given the topic, one pupil is the boxer who will deliver the 'blows'. The other members are the boxing coaches who help the boxer win the fight by researching and helping to prepare the boxer (speaker).

• Discuss the controversy surrounding boxing; although it is an ancient sport requiring high levels of strength, fitness and skill, many people are against this sport in which people inflict blows to the head and body of an opponent with the intent to cause harm (which can lead to cause serious injuries, especially to the brain).

• Find out who the Irish champions for each weight division are.

Boxing

Boxing—hitting an opponent with the fists—is an ancient sport that has been part of the modern Olympics since 1904. The 2012 Olympics sees the introduction of women's boxing to the Games.

Boxers compete in a raised square platform area called a **ring**. The ring has a padded post in each corner and four covered ropes connecting the posts. Posts have certain colours: red (in the near corner to the left of the president of the jury), blue (far right-side corner) and white (in the far left-side and near right corners). Prior to a match (called a bout), each boxer is assigned a corner that is referred to as either the red corner or blue corner. A boxer wears either blue or red clothes and padded gloves (to minimise damage to his/her fists and opponent) depending on the colour of his/her corner. The opponent wears the opposite colour, while the referee wears white.

Boxers fight opponents who are about the same weight as they are. The weight divisions have different names. For men, they are: light flyweight (<48 kg), flyweight (<51 kg), bantamweight (<54 kg), lightweight (<60 kg), light welterweight (<64 kg), welterweight (<69 kg), middleweight (<75 kg), light heavyweight (<81 kg), heavyweight (<91 kg) and super heavyweight (>91 kg). For women: flyweight (<51 kg), lightweight (57–60 kg) and middleweight (69–75 kg).

Boxers must have the same types of gloves. These have a white strip across the knuckle. When a boxer hits the opponent with this white section, on the front or sides of the opponent's body (above the belt) or head, judges give him or her one point. The winner of the bout is the boxer with the most points.

1. Colour the red and blue posts, and the helmet, clothing and gloves of each boxer in the picture above.

2. Why are the gloves are padded? _____

_____

3. What would happen (in boxing weight divisions) to a male flyweight boxer who gained four kilograms?

_____

4. How can a boxer score a point in an Olympic bout?

_____

_____

cycling

objective

- Reads and comprehends information about the sport of cycling at the 2012 Games.

teacher information

- Four disciplines make up the sport of cycling at the Olympics: BMX, mountain bike, road and track.

- There has been at least one cycling discipline featured at every modern Olympic Games since 1896 in Athens. Road cycling for men was on the programme in 1896. It was dropped for the next two Games and reintroduced in 1912 in Stockholm. Women first participated in road cycling at the 1984 Games in Los Angeles. Track cycling for men has been at all but the 1912 Olympic Games. Women's track cycling has been included since the 1988 Olympic Games in Seoul. Mountain bike has been on the Olympic programme for men and women since 1996 in Atlanta. BMX was first introduced for both men and women at the 2008 Beijing Olympic Games.

- Listed below are the four cycling discipline webpages for the London Games that pupils can use to complete page 81. Use these pages and click on the links under the heading 'Other sites' on each webpage to find facts about each discipline:

  – <http://www.london2012.com/cycling-bmx>

  – <http://www.london2012.com/cycling-mountain-bike>

  – <http://www.london2012.com/cycling-road>

  – <http://www.london2012.com/cycling-track>.

- The following sports schedule website gives accurate information about the events in each discipline:

  <http://www.london2012.com/olympic-schedule>

answers

Page 81

BMX: individual event for men and one for women; seeding races, quarter-finals, semi-finals, final/one gear, one brake, strong to handle landings from jumps but light for speed/padded all-in-one suits, gloves, knee and elbow pads, helmet with face mask, reinforced shoes

Mountain bike: outdoor course at Hadleigh Farm; rough, hilly countryside with rocks, climbs and descents/one individual race for men and one for women, mass start, no heats/tight-fitting, all-in-one suits; gloves; helmet; cycle shoes

Track: Velodrome in Olympic Park, inside oval-shaped track that banks steeply all around/no brakes (to keep bike light), rigid lightweight frame, thin tyres/tight-fitting, all-in-one suits; gloves, special streamlined helmet, cycle shoes attached to pedals

Road: The Mall for road races, Hampton Court for time trials; courses on existing roads/individual road race and time trial for men, and same for women/range of gears and brakes, light and fast

additional activities

- Pupils can share their answers for the heading 'Another fact' in the retrieval chart on page 81.

- Use a search engine to find suitable photographs to view of the various bikes used with each discipline. Along with the information gathered for page 81, compare the similarities and differences among the four bikes. Provide explanations for the differences; e.g. there are no brakes on a track bike so as to keep the bike lighter.

- For each webpage, use the links under the 'Teacher information' section to view the nations and individuals who have won medals in the various disciplines.

Cycling

The sport of cycling will feature in four disciplines at the Olympic Games: BMX, mountain bike, track and road. There are events for men and women in all disciplines.

Use the webpages your teacher suggests to complete the chart with facts about each discipline. Some facts have already been summarised for you.

	Description of venue/course	Event(s)	Description of bike	Description of clothing	Another fact
BMX	outdoor track next to Velodrome in Olympic Park dirt track built up with jumps, tightly-banked corners and obstacles				
Mountain bike			extra suspension; excellent braking system; built for sturdiness, speed, durability and comfort		
Track		five for men and five for women team pursuit, team sprint, individual sprint, keirin, omnium			
Road				tight-fitting, all-in-one suits; gloves; helmet (streamlined for time trials); cycle shoes attached to pedals	

equestrian

objective

- Reads and comprehends information about the sport of equestrian at the 2012 Games.

teacher information

- Equestrian events will be held in Greenwich Park on the south bank of the Thames in south-east London. The cross-country course will incorporate the use of natural obstacles as well as artificial ones. Trees and shrubs will be pruned if necessary, but none will be removed.

- Equestrian events first appeared on the Olympic programme in Paris in 1900, then were withdrawn until the Games in Stockholm in 1912. Until the 1948 Olympic Games in London, only men competed as riders and they had to be officers in the military. This ban had been lifted by the Helsinki 1952 Olympic Games when civilians, including women, could participate.

- Dressage is considered the artful discipline of equestrian sport and requires great skill and concentration from both horse and rider. The fundamental purpose of dressage is to develop a horse's athletic ability and willingness to perform. The horse needs to respond to a rider's commands while making it appear effortless. The appearance and grooming of horse and rider are important. Horses have braided manes, banged (cut off blunt at the bottom) and pulled (trimmed to shape by pulling out hairs) tails, trimmed legs and polished hooves. Riders are formally dressed in white breeches, a white shirt, a stock tie with a gold pin, a top hat to match their coat, white gloves, tall boots and spurs. Long hair is usually worn in a hair net.

bold words

- Sort the words used to complete the cloze into alphabetical order and show the syllable breaks for each word:

  con/sists, cross-/coun/try, dress/age,
  in/di/vid/u/al, high/est, known, mu/sic,
  ob/sta/cles, past, re/fus/es, same, streams, three,
  through/out, trot

answers

1. three	2. individual	3. same
4. consists	5. trot	6. music
7. highest	8. known	9. obstacles
10. refuses	11. past	12. dressage
13. throughout	14. cross-country	15. streams

additional activity

- Compose acrostic poems about each discipline in equestrian by using each letter in the names of the three disciplines of dressage, jumping and eventing to start a new line of the poem.

- View images on television of riders in various equestrian events while the London 2012 Olympic Games is in progress to learn more about the sport. The following webpage can also be used:

  – <http://www.london2012.com/equestrian-dressage>

  – <http://www.london2012.com/equestrian-jumping>

  – <http://www.london2012.com/equestrian-eventing>

Note: There are further websites to view from links on these webpages. Look for the links in the bottom right-hand corner of the pages.

Equestrian

Complete the cloze to find out about the sport of equestrian for men and women at the Games in London.

dressage	individual	obstacles	trot	streams
three	past	consists	music	cross-country
refuses	highest	same	known	throughout

Equestrian consists of _____ [1] separate disciplines: dressage, jumping and eventing. There are team and _____ [2] events in each discipline. It is the only Olympic sport in which men and women compete on equal terms, in exactly the _____ [3] events. Dressage has been described as 'horse ballet'. It _____ [4] of a series of compulsory movements within a flat, rectangular arena. Horses perform graceful stepping movements at a walk, _____ [5] or canter pace on their riders' commands. Dressage tests the obedience and willingness of the horse. All riders complete two rounds in their national teams—both set by equestrian authorities. After this part, the team with the most points is the winner and receives the gold medal. However, this is not the end as the best individual performers in the team event go on to perform a third routine set to _____ [6], which they choreograph themselves. The winner of the individual event is the rider who scores the _____ [7] points during the final round. Jumping is also _____ [8] as 'show jumping'. It takes place around a short course containing 12 to 14 _____ [9] called 'fences'. Riders and their horses attempt to jump the fences in a specific order under a set time. Horses are challenged with water jumps, vertical jumps and double and treble jumps. Different penalty points are given if a horse _____ [10] a jump or knocks a fence down, if a rider falls, or the jumps are completed _____ [11] the set time. Again, team and individual events are combined, and the winner(s) is/are the rider(s) with the fewest penalty points. Eventing is held over four days and combines _____ [12], jumping and a third part called cross-country. Each competitor rides the same horse _____ [13] the competition. The _____ [14] course is held over several kilometres of open space containing up to 45 jumps. These include fallen trees, stone walls, _____ [15] and ditches. Again, the team event is completed earlier, with the top riders then competing in the individual round. The winner is the rider with the fewest penalty points.

fencing

objective

- Reads information and completes activities about fencing.

teacher information

- Fencing was part of the first Olympics Games in 1896. Epée and sabre events have been held at every Summer Olympics.

- Fencing bouts take place on a long narrow strip called a 'piste', which is 14 metres long and 1.5 to 2 metres wide. A bout is controlled by a referee. An electronic apparatus is used to detect when a fencer makes a hit, and the referee then decides whether a score should be awarded.

- Fencers often specialise in one of the three different swords in fencing (the epée, foil, and sabre). Each sword differs in how it is used to score hits. With foil and epée, only a thrust with the point of the weapon scores, while the side and edge of the sabre can be used for a hit.

- At international events, refereeing is in French. A system of corresponding hand gestures from the referee accompanies the spoken commands. The fencing competitors must start and stop on the referee's commands.

bold words

- The three words in bold print are the weapons used in modern fencing.

answers

1. The following words should be circled in the text:

   (a) piste   (b) the torso   (c) the sabre   (d) bout   (e) bell guard   (f) en-guarde line   (g) mask

2. Pupils should be able to draw a scale diagram of the piste using the images and information provided, drawing in centimetres (drawing a 14 cm x 2 cm rectangle to represent the 14 m x 2 m piste). An example of a piste diagram is as follows:

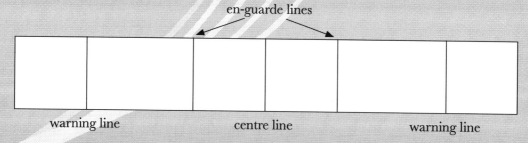

en-guarde lines

warning line   centre line   warning line

additional activities

- The piste is made of a conductive surface such as copper mesh or aluminium plate. Pupils could find out more about conductive materials.

- Discuss the sentence in the first paragraph, 'Modern fencing has terminology and formalities that reflect its long history'. Which parts of the sport of fencing reflect its history? Research the origin of the clothing, formalities (such as saluting) and French words used in fencing.

- Watch a film such as *The Three Musketeers* (or a section of an age-appropriate film with a fencing scene) and discuss the fencing. How are they similar to, or different from, modern fencing bouts? What kind of swords were used in the film?

Fencing

Fencing is an ancient form of sword fighting that has been an Olympic sport since the Games began. Modern fencing has terminology and formalities that reflect its long history.

The aim of fencing is to try to score hits on the opponent with a sword. Three kinds of swords are used:

The **epée** is the heaviest sword. It has a stiff blade and a large bell guard to protect the hand.	The **sabre** has a light, flat blade and a knuckle guard.	The **foil** is a light, flexible weapon with a blunted point.
Points are scored with the tip of the blade on any part of the head, torso, arms, legs, or feet.	Points can be scored with the tip, edges and sides of the blade anywhere above the opponent's waist.	Points are scored only with the tip of the blade on the torso of the opponent.

The contest (a bout) is competed on an area called a piste. It is 1.5 to 2 metres wide and 14 metres long. Crossing the piste are a number of lines: a centre line, two en-garde lines (2 m either side of the centre) and a warning line (2 m from either end of the strip) to let a fencer know that he or she is nearly out of room with which to fight.

A fencer wears protective trousers, gloves, a jacket and mask. A bout starts with the fencers, masks off, saluting each other and the referee. They put on their masks and adopt the fencing stance at the en-garde line as the referee calls *'En-garde!'*, then *'Prêt?'* (Ready?) and *'Allez!'* (Play!) Hits are usually scored electronically through a cord or cable that runs from the weapon, through their jacket, to a nearby scoring apparatus.

1. Circle words in the text to answer each of the questions below.

(a) The area on which a fencing competition takes place.

(b) The part of the body on which a foil can score points.

(c) The sword that can score with the edges and sides of its blade.

(d) The name given to a fencing match.

(e) The protective part of the epée.

(f) Where the fencers stand at the beginning of a bout.

(g) The item worn by a fencer to protect his or her head.

2. On the back of this sheet, draw a scale drawing of the piste, labelling the centre, en-guarde and warning lines.

football

objective

- Reads and demonstrates understanding of text by identifying facts and opinions.

teacher information

- During the Games, a number of Olympic football matches are usually played in a city some distance from the host city and this will be happening again in 2012. From 25 July to 11 August, six venues will be hosting Olympic football matches. These include: one venue in Scotland (Hampden Park in Glasgow), one in Wales (Millennium Stadium in Cardiff), one in Manchester (Old Trafford), one in Newcastle-upon-Tyne (St James' Park) one in Coventry (City of Coventry) as well as Wembley Stadium in north-west London, where both gold medals will be decided.

- There will be 16 men's teams and 12 women's teams competing in groups of four, then eight teams will play in the quarter-finals. Each team fields 11 players, along with six substitutes. A round football is used and each team tries to score goals while defending its own goal. Players can use any part of their body except their hands, arms and shoulders; so the ball can't be thrown or caught while in play. Players are very skilful at dribbling the ball along the ground, bouncing it on or off their feet and legs and at 'heading' the ball. Many goals are the result of a ball being propelled into a goal from a player's head.

- Football has been played in every Olympiad except 1896 and 1932, but it wasn't until 1908 that a proper international competition was organised at the Games (by the Football Association). Great Britain won the gold medal, as they did again in 1912. Women's football was first played in 1996. Football has been controversial at the Olympics because of the once-standing ruling that only amateurs could compete. This meant that most of the world's best footballers were ineligible. The rule was changed for the Los Angeles Games in 1984.

- Under the current rules (introduced so teams would compete on a more equal footing), some strong football nations have unimpressive Olympic records. The current rules state that all but three players in a men's football team must be under 23 years of age—making many of the world's best players, and those fans would most want to watch play, ineligible. This may explain why Olympic football doesn't evoke the same interest and passion as the World Cup, which features the world's best footballers.

- As the host country, a football team from Great Britain automatically qualifies for the football competition. This has caused great controversy because England, Wales, Scotland and Northern Ireland all have separate teams in the World Cup and the Northern Irish, Welsh and Scottish FAs are concerned that fielding just one team with members from all four football associations could jeopardise their future position with the international football committee, FIFA. The compromise was that Team Great Britain would only have English players. This was agreed to, but some players from Scotland, Wales and Northern Ireland have objected. It's an issue that will not be easily settled.

answers

1. (a) O   (b) F   (c) O   (d) F
   (e) O   (f) O   (g) O   (h) F
   (i) F   (j) O   (k) F   (l) F
2.–3. Teacher check

additional activities

- Choose a city which has hosted an Olympic Games and research to find other cities in that country where some of the football matches were played. Draw a map of the country, showing the host and the other cities.

- Research a famous male footballer and write a persuasive letter saying why he should be included in his country's Olympic football team.

Football

1. Read the information about Olympic football. Indicate which statements are facts and which are opinions by writing F or O in the boxes.

   (a) Playing football matches at one Games venue in Scotland, one in Wales and four in England will make Olympic football more interesting. ☐

   (b) Both the women's and the men's gold medal football matches will be played at Wembley Stadium in London. ☐

   (c) There will be 16 men's teams and only 12 women's teams competing because the men's games are more spectacular. ☐

   (d) The first women's football game will be played on 25 July, which is before the Opening Ceremony, and the men's gold medal match will be played on 11 August. ☐

   (e) Football is a hard game to play because you can't touch the ball with your hands, arms or shoulders while it is in play. ☐

   (f) It is not easy to learn how to use your head to hit the ball into the net to score a goal. ☐

   (g) If you want to play football well you must practise 'dribbling', which is using your feet to move the ball along the ground. ☐

   (h) Until the Olympics in Los Angeles in 1984, only amateurs were allowed to compete in the Games. ☐

   (i) In every men's Olympic football team, only three of the players can be over 23 years of age. ☐

   (j) The under–23 rule should be changed because most of the best football players in the world are too old to play in the Olympics. ☐

   (k) More people around the world watch the football World Cup than the Olympic football games. ☐

   (l) It is expected that there will be 2400 footballs used at football matches during the Games. ☐

2. Which do you think is the most interesting fact?

   _____

   _____

3. Write about your own opinion of Olympic football.

   _____

   _____

   _____

gymnastics

objective

- Reads and comprehends information about the sport of gymnastics at the 2012 Games.

teacher information

- Three disciplines make up the sport of gymnastics: artistic gymnastics, rhythmic gymnastics and trampoline.

answers

Page 89

1. Men: six apparatus, parallel bars, rings, horizontal bar, pommel horse, vault 135 cm high, no music to accompany floor routine, first competed at 1896 Games

   Women: four apparatus, balance beam, uneven bars, vault 125 cm high, floor routine accompanied by music, first competed at 1928 Games

   Both: floor, vault, individual and team events, scoring system the same

2. floor: series of backward and forward jumps, leaps, somersaults and twists (women's to music)

   vault: gymnasts run toward the vault, take off from a springboard in front of it and push off the vault with two hands to make acrobatic moves before landing on both feet

   pommel horse: using only hands for support, gymnasts perform continuous swinging and circular motions with their upper body and legs

   rings: gymnasts perform a routine requiring stillness of the body between movements while holding onto two parallel wooden rings suspended from straps

   parallel bars: swinging, vaulting and balancing routine

   horizontal bar: swinging routine with various grips, releases and re-grasps of the bar

   beam: forward and backward tumbling moves, turns, leaps and jumps

   uneven bars: routine of complex swinging movements with grip changes, releases and new grasps

Page 90

1. women	2. dance	3. measuring
4. routine	5. individual	6. ball
7. bounces	8. hand	9. two
10. weigh	11. both	12. attached
13. spirals	14. hoop	15. variety

Page 91

Possible answers:

(a) All 16 trampolinists perform a compulsory routine and an optional routine in a qualifying round. Those with the eight highest scores make it through to the final.

(b) The trampolinist might have moved too far from the centre of the trampoline or not maintained height in the air.

(c) They need to be as high in the air as they can so there is time to perform as many skills as possible before landing.

additional activities

- Follow the individual and team artistic gymnastic, rhythmic gymnastic and trampoline competitions and work out how the scores are given and the eventual winners are determined. Compare the similarities and differences among each discipline.

- Use the following websites to find out about some of the moves trampolinists perform: adolph, rudolph, barani, fliffis, quadriffis and randolph.

  - <http://www.london2012.com/gymnastics-trampoline>

  - <http://www.olympic.org/trampoline-equipment-and-history>

  - <http://assets.olympic.org/SportAnimations/en/summer/GT/GT_EN.html>

Artistic gymnastics

Artistic gymnastics is one of the three disciplines in the sport of gymnastics at the Olympic Games. Gymnasts use a variety of apparatus to perform highly skilled exercises.

1. Read the following information about artistic gymnastics then sort as many facts as you can into the correct place in the Venn diagram.

- Men and women will compete in individual and team events. Men have participated since the first modern Olympic Games in 1896, while women first competed at the 1928 Games in Amsterdam.

- Men compete on six apparatus: floor, vault, pommel horse, rings, parallel bars and horizontal bar. Women compete on four apparatus: floor, vault, balance beam and uneven bars. Unlike the men, the women's floor routine is accompanied by music. The vault used by women is 125 cm in height, while the men's is 135 cm.

- A group of judges award each gymnast a score for each performance based on the degree of difficulty and the quality of the performance.

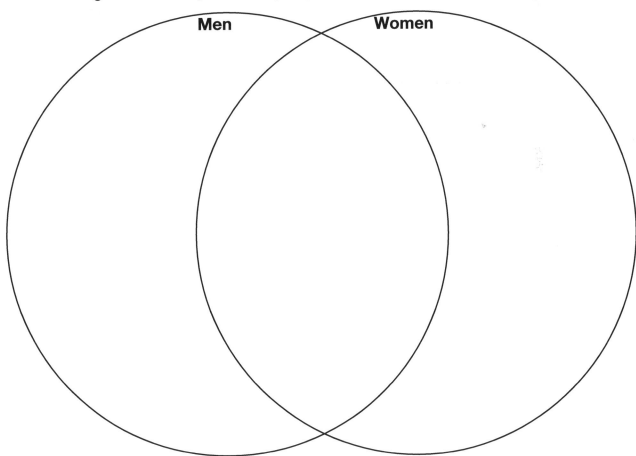

Men   **Women**

2. Use the following websites and others you find to summarise the routine a gymnast performs on each apparatus.

<http://www.london2012.com/gymnastics-artistic>

<http://www.olympic.org/artistic-gymnastics-equipment-and-history>

<http://assets.olympic.org/SportAnimations/en/summer/GA/GA_EN.html>

Rhythmic gymnastics

Complete the cloze to find out about rhythmic gymnastics, one of the three disciplines in the sport of gymnastics at the London Games.

Rhythmic gymnastics is one of two sports in which only _____¹ participate at the Olympic Games (the other is synchronised swimming). The sport combines gymnastics with _____². Gymnasts perform spectacular routines to music using hand apparatus: ball, hoop, ribbon and clubs.

Each routine is conducted on a floor area _____³ 13 m by 13 m. The apparatus must be in constant motion throughout the routine, be handled with as much variety as possible and with fluid movements. During a one minute and 30 second-long _____⁴, gymnasts leap, jump and pivot at the same time as using the apparatus. There are _____⁵ and team events.

The _____⁶ is made of rubber or a synthetic material and is 18 to 20 cm in diameter. As the ball is the only apparatus without an easy grip, gymnasts cannot make the slightest error. During the routine, the gymnast throws, catches, _____,⁷ swings and rolls the ball over her body. As the ball cannot be gripped, it must be captured in the palm of the _____⁸.

The _____⁹ clubs used are bottle-shaped and made of wood or a synthetic material. They are 40 to 50 cm long and _____¹⁰ 150 g. As clubs are thrown and caught by the left and right hands, gymnasts that are ambidextrous (able to use _____¹¹ hands equally well) have an advantage.

The 7 m ribbon is made of satin or a similar material. It is _____¹² to a 50 to 60 cm–long rod. Considered to be the most graceful apparatus, gymnasts perform large and free-flowing movements in the form of _____¹³ and figure-eight shapes.

The _____¹⁴ is made of wood or plastic and has a diameter of between 80 to 90 cm. This apparatus offers the widest _____¹⁵ of movements and technical skills. The gymnast must make at least three leaps with the hoop.

routine	individual	variety	spirals	both
attached	weigh	women	bounces	measuring
ball	hoop	two	dance	hand

Trampoline

Trampoline is one of the three disciplines in the sport of gymnastics. It has been a part of gymnastics at the Olympic Games since Sydney in 2000. Men and women compete only in individual events at Olympic Games.

The competition consists of two parts: a qualification round and the final round. In the qualification round, trampolinists perform a compulsory routine of set skills followed by an optional routine of 10 different skills of the competitor's choice. Scores from each routine are added for an overall score. The top eight trampolinists qualify for the final. Scores are not carried over to the final. Finalists perform another optional routine of 10 other different skills. Judges award scores to competitors in all routines based on the degree of difficulty and execution of the jumps and skills displayed. More difficult moves receive higher scores. Marks are deducted for errors such as moving too far from the centre of the trampoline or not maintaining height above the apparatus.

Trampolinists bounce to get to the correct height before commencing their routine. Because they want to perform as many skills as possible between each bounce, they need to be high in the air—as much as 10 metres for as long as two seconds. The multiple somersaults and twists the trampolinists execute should be performed continuously and without hesitation.

The final landing on the trampoline must be steady and controlled, with both feet on the trampoline bed. The trampolinist must remain upright for three seconds to prove stability. During the routine, feet and legs must be kept together (except in straddle moves) and feet and toes pointed. Socks or gym shoes can be worn.

Imagine you are watching the finals of the competition with a friend. Answer his or her questions.

(a) 'The announcer said there were 16 trampolinists at the start of the competition. What happened to the other eight?'

_____

_____

_____

(b) 'One of the judges took marks off that trampolinist for a mistake. The landing was perfect. I wonder what the judge could have noticed to deduct marks?'

_____

_____

(c) 'I wonder why they jump so high—it looks scary!'

_____

_____

OLYMPIC COUNCIL
OF IRELAND

hockey

objective

- Reads and demonstrates understanding of a text by selecting keywords in specified categories and using this information to write a paragraph about one of the categories.

teacher information

- It is believed that the name 'hockey' originated from the French word 'hocquet', the name of a type of shepherd's crook. This is because the game is played with a crook-shaped stick. Forms of what we now call hockey have been played since 2000 BCE and it is believed to be the oldest ball game played at the Olympics. The Amateur Hockey Association of London was formed in 1886 and men's hockey first featured at the 1908 Olympics. However, women's hockey didn't make its Olympic debut until the 1980 Games in Moscow. Traditionally the game has been played on grass, but this all changed after water-based synthetic turf was introduced in 1976 at Montreal. The game then became much faster.

- Hockey is played on an outdoor pitch by two teams of 11 players using a hard white plastic ball which can travel at speeds of up to 120 km/h. There are two 35-minute halves. Protective equipment is worn by outfield players in the form of shin pads, but goalies require helmets, and thick leg and elbow pads. Players wear shoes with grip but goalies, who are permitted to kick the ball, wear special 'kickers' for this purpose. Umpires control games and can issue infringement cards. A green card is a warning and the player leaves the pitch for two minutes; a yellow card results in a longer suspension; and a player who is given a red card takes no further part in the game.

- The new Hockey Centre, situated in the north of Olympic Park, is the venue for all hockey games. There are two pitches at this temporary venue: one with seating for 16 000 where all games will be played, and a warm-up pitch. At the conclusion of the Games, these two pitches will be moved to Eton Manor, north of Olympic Park. Training facilities will be provided during the Games at the Old Loughtonians Hockey Club in Essex, where two identical Olympic pitches will be available. For the first time, games will be played on blue pitches with pink run-off areas. It is anticipated that the white ball and lines will be easier for spectators at matches (and for those watching on television) to see.

- There will be 12 teams of 16 players each competing for the men's and the women's gold medals. Each event will be played in two pools of six teams over 14 days from 29 July to the gold medal events on 11 August. Seventy-six matches of hockey will be played in total.

- Visit <http://www.london2012.com/hockey> to view a short introductory video of men's and women's hockey and <http://www.olympic.org/hockey> to watch a video of the 2008 women's final between the Netherlands and China.

answers

Teacher check

additional activities

- Write two facts and two opinions about the game of hockey.

- In a small group, discuss the skills a hockey player needs and compile a list. Decide the importance of each skill and rank them accordingly. Compare your ranked list with those of other groups.

- Research an Olympic hockey player and write a biography.

Hockey

Versions of hockey have been played for thousands of years. Nowadays, it is played outdoors by teams of 11 men or women. They use a stick with a hook on one end and try to score goals by hitting a hard white plastic ball into a net at the opponents' end of the pitch. A game is played in two halves of 35 minutes and at half-time the teams change ends. Until synthetic turf was introduced in the 1970s, hockey was played on grass. Although many hockey games around the world are still played on grass, elite hockey is usually played on a synthetic surface. Since the introduction of smoother synthetic turf, hockey has become a much faster game.

Olympic men's hockey was first played more than 100 years ago, in 1908. It took 72 years before women's hockey was introduced at the Moscow Games. Hockey is played in many countries, but it is particularly popular in the United Kingdom, India, Pakistan, Australia, the Netherlands, Germany and Spain. Because ice hockey is a Winter Olympic sport, hockey played at the Summer Olympics is sometimes referred to as 'field hockey' to distinguish the two.

The new Hockey Centre has been constructed in Olympic Park specifically for the Games. The view across Olympic Park from this venue will be stunning. Located at the centre will be two blue hockey pitches with pink run-offs. One of these colourful pitches will have seats for 16 000 spectators. The other (identical) pitch will only be used for warming up. Organisers believe these unique blue pitches will make it easier for players and spectators, and viewers around the world, to see the white ball and lines on the pitch. There will be 76 hockey matches played by the 12 men's and the 12 women's teams competing for gold at the Games. Hockey will start on 29 July and will continue for 14 days. After the Games, the two pitches will be moved to Eton Manor and set up with 3000 permanent seats. These are able to be increased to 15 000 for any future major hockey events.

1. **(a)** Write keywords and numbers from the text to record information about hockey and the Olympics in each of the columns below.

Olympic hockey history	The game of hockey	The Olympic venue	The Olympic competition

(b) Use the information in one of the columns to write a paragraph.

sailing

OBJECTIVE

- Uses information read about sailing to complete activities.

TEACHER INFORMATION

- The sailing events at the 2012 Summer Olympics will take place at Weymouth and Portland in the county of Dorset, England.

- Sailing was first competed at the Olympics in 1900 and has been a part of the Games since (with the exception of 1904). The sailing classes have changed slightly since the previous Olympic sailing events in Beijing in 2008. Ten different sailing events (six for men, four for women) will be competed at the Olympics in 2012, with a variety of craft being used.

- Points in each of a series of sailing races are awarded according to position. First place is awarded one point, second place two points, and so on. The final race is called the medal race, for which points are doubled. The individual or crew with the fewest total points after the medal race is the winner. Most races are fleet races, with all competitors starting together and racing against each other. The Elliott 6-metre women's event will be a match race. Match racing is one against one and involves strategy and tactics.

BOLD WORDS

- The words in bold print are the different boats that will be sailed at the Olympics in 2012. The pupils will need to use these words to complete the labelling activity (Question 1).

ANSWERS

1. Boats from left to right: RS:X, Laser Radial, Laser, Finn, 470, 49er, Elliott 6-metre, Star.

2.

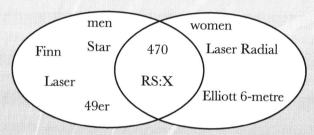

ADDITIONAL ACTIVITIES

- Pupils investigate the functions of the different parts of a sail boat, such as the different sails, the keel and the rudder. Discuss the forces that act on these parts of the boat.

- Have a series of contests in the classroom, scoring them as a sailing event is scored, with the winner being the person with the least amount of points.

- Compare:

  – the way the different keels work. Rate the keels according to their ability to be easily manoeuvred and the stability they provide

  – sailing boats to other kinds of boats, focussing on the different methods of propulsion

  – the boats being used in this Olympic Games to boats raced at past Games.

Sailing

Sailing has been a part of most Summer Olympic Games since they began. Over time, different classes (types of sailboats based on their hulls, keels and sails) have been used in competition at the Olympics. At the Summer Games in 2012, there are 10 different events (six men's and four women's):

The **Finn** has one large, adjustable mainsail. To sail a Finn requires strength, concentration and quick reflexes. The Finn will be raced by men in 2012.

The **Laser** (standard) sailboat is a popular small sailing dinghy with one sail. It is sailed by one person and will be used in a men's event at the Olympics.

The **Laser Radial** has the same hull as the Laser, but has a smaller sail and shorter mast. Used by one person, Laser Radial racing will be a women's event in 2012.

The **470** has a mainsail and a small jib and spinnaker. The name comes from the length of the boat (470 centimetres). The 470 has been sailed in the Olympics since 1976. It is light and maneuverable and sailed by two people. The dinghy will be used by men and women in separate events in 2012.

The **49er** is the fastest Olympic team boat. It has a mainsail, jib, low hull and large spinnaker, and an adjustable wing on each side of the boat. Two people sail the 49er, which will be used in a men's event in 2012.

The **Elliott 6-metre** will be raced at the Olympics for the first time in 2012. It has a long, thin keel with a bulb at the end; a large mainsail; a jib and spinnaker; and is crewed by three. It will be used for women's match racing at the Games.

The largest boat is the **Star** keelboat. It has a wide keel and a huge mainsail on a long boom. It will be used in competition by two-men teams in 2012.

The **RS:X** is a type of windsurfer. It has one sail and a small, thin hull. It will be used in competition by men and women in separate events.

1. Label the eight sailboats below using the words in bold in the text above.

2. Fill in the Venn diagram, showing which events will be sailed by men only, women only and both men and women.

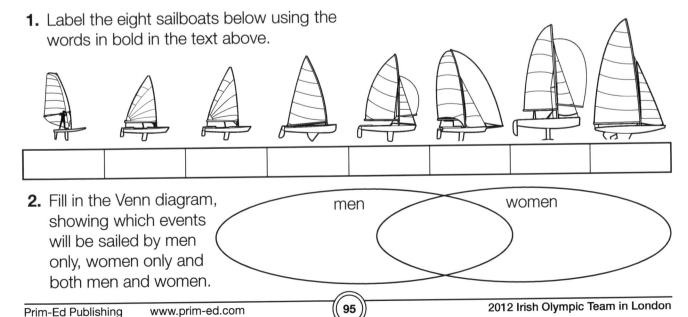

OLYMPIC COUNCIL OF IRELAND

shooting

objectives

- Answers questions to show understanding of the different shooting events.
- Researches to find comprehensive details of a single shooting event.

teacher information

- Pierre de Coubertin, founder of the modern Olympic Games, was a champion shooter in his youth and shooting events have been a part of all but two (1904, 1928) of the Modern Olympics Games. Initially there were just three events, but in London there are 15. Women began competing in shooting events at the 1984 Games in Los Angeles.
- In 1908, clay pigeons were introduced to replace live pigeons as targets.
- The governing body of the shooting sports event is the International Shooting Sport Federation.

answers

1. *Men only:* 25 m rapid fire pistol, 50 m pistol, 50 m rifle prone, shotgun double trap

   Women only: 25 m pistol

   Men and women: 10 m air pistol, 10 m air rifle, 50 m rifle three positions, skeet, trap

2. *Rifle and pistol:* shoot at ten-ringed target; shoot from distances of 10 m and 50 m

   Rifle and shotgun: two competitions for men and women, one competition for men only; fire with both hands using shoulder for support

3. The trap releases only one target at a time while the double trap releases two. The double trap targets are released from the same location, while those for the skeet events are launched from two separate locations.

4. (a) 2700   (b) 1300

additional activities

- Write a detailed report on a shooting event. Include sketches of equipment and other diagrams to clarify information. Explain scoring and rules.
- For each shooting event, find the gold, silver and bronze medallists from the Olympics in 2008. Draw up a table with their names and flags of the nations they represent. Leave a space in the table to record the medal winners from the London Games.

Shooting

In the sport of shooting, there are five events for each of the three firearms used.

All competitions consist of a qualification and a final round. Scores for each round are added up to give a total score which identifies the winner.

Pistol	Rifle	Shotgun
The pistol is fired from standing position.	The rifle is fired from standing, kneeling or prone positions.	The shotgun is fired from standing position.
Only one hand is used to fire.	Both firearms require both hands to fire. The shoulder is used for support.	
The shooter aims at a ten-ringed target from the given distance: 10, 25 or 50 metres. Hitting the inner ring scores 10 and the outer ring scores 1.		The shooter aims at clay targets that have been launched at different angles by a machine called a 'trap'. A point is awarded for each target hit. Two shots are allowed for each target. In the double trap competition, targets are launched two at a time from the same trap. In the skeet, targets are launched from two separate towers—one on either side of the range. In the double trap and skeet, one shot per target is allowed.
10 metre air pistol (60 shots for men, 40 shots for women; plus 10 shots in final)	*10 metre air rifle* (60 shots for men, 40 shots for women; plus 10 shots in final)	*skeet* (125 targets for men, 75 targets for women; plus 25 targets in final)
25 metre pistol (60 shots for women only, plus 20 shots in final)	*50 metre rifle 3 positions* (3 x 40 shots for men, 3 x 20 shots for women; plus 10 shots in final)	*trap* (125 targets for men, 75 targets for women; plus 25 targets in final)
25 metre rapid fire pistol (60 shots for men only, plus 20 shots in final) *50 metre pistol* (60 shots for men only, plus 10 shots in final)	*50 metre rifle prone* (60 shots for men only, plus 10 shots in final)	*double trap* (120 targets for men only, plus 50 targets in final)

Write answers on the back of the worksheet.

1. Draw a Venn diagram to show the events competed in by men only, women only and men and women.

2. In a table, show the similarities between the rifle and pistol events, and the rifle and shotgun events.

3. Describe the differences between the trap, double trap and skeet.

4. (a) If a male competitor took part in all the rifle events, what is the maximum score he could possibly make?

   (b) If a female competitor took part in all the pistol events, what is the maximum score she could possibly make?